A NEW GERMANY
IN A NEW EUROPE

TODD HERZOG AND SANDER L. GILMAN
EDITORS

ROUTLEDGE
NEW YORK LONDON

Published in 2001 by
Routledge
29 West 35th Street
New York, NY 10001

Published in Great Britain by
Routledge
11 New Fetter Lane
London EC4P 4EE

10 9 8 7 6 5 4 3 2 1

Library of Congress Cataloging-in-Publication Data

A new Germany in a new Europe / edited by Todd Herzog and Sander L. Gilman.
    p. cm.
Papers from a conference held at the University of Chicago, June 9–10, 1999.
Includes bibliographical references and index.
ISBN 0-415-92807-9 (alk. paper)–ISBN 0-415-92808-7 (alk. paper : pbk.)
1. Germany–Cultural policy. 2. Germany–Social conditions–1990– 3. Germany
Ethnic relations. 4. Germany–Relations–Europe. 5. Europe–Relations–Germany. I.
Herzog, Todd. II. Gilman, Sander L.

DD290.26 .N48 2000
943.087–dc21
                                                        00-036891

Dedicated to

Michael Engelhard

Scholar, Diplomat, and Friend of Chicago

CONTENTS

INTRODUCTION

Sander L. Gilman   1

　　Two Hundred and Fifty Years after Goethe's Birth,
　　Fifty Years after the Aspen Conference, Ten Years
　　after Reunification

CAN GOETHE GUIDE US THROUGH THE PROCESS OF
EUROPEAN UNION?

Richard von Weizsäcker   25

WHAT IS THE FUTURE OF GERMAN IMMIGRATION POLICY?

Barbara John   43

　　German Immigration Policy—Past, Present, and Future

Saskia Sassen   49

　　Beyond Sovereignty: De facto Transnationalism in
　　Immigration Policy

WHAT IS THE PLACE OF GERMAN CULTURE WITHIN TODAY'S
EUROPEAN CULTURE?

Peter Schneider   77

　　The Federal Republic of Germany Turns Fifty

Helmut Müller-Sievers   89

　　The Humboldt-Goethe Complex

HOW DIVERSE IS THE GERMAN CULTURAL MARKET?

Henryk Broder   **99**
    Reshuffling the Deck: Democratization and
    Diversification of the Cultural Market

Dagmar C. G. Lorenz   **105**
    Beyond Goethe: Perspectives on Postunification
    German Literature

DOES THE NEW NATIONAL GERMAN CINEMA HAVE AN AUDIENCE?

Monika Treut   **117**
    Between National Television and International
    Oblivion: German Cinema in the 1990s

David Levin   **131**
    This Cinema That Is Not One? Monika Treut and
    a Deterritorialized German Cinema

WHAT ARE THE SITES OF MEMORY AND MEMORIALIZATION TODAY
AND WHAT SHOULD THEY DO?

Tom L. Freudenheim   **143**
    Confronting Memory and Museums

Howard A. Sulkin   **167**
    The Task of Museums

CONCLUSION

Andreas Glaeser   **173**
    Why Germany Remains Divided

Contributors   199
Index   201

INTRODUCTION

Two Hundred and Fifty Years after Goethe's Birth,
Fifty Years after the Aspen Conference,
Ten Years after Reunification

Sander L. Gilman

Germany as a nation, wrote the American novelist Ward Just, born in Chicago of German ancestry, "resembled Chicago, central to its region, a furious engine that advances on its own inner logic, closed in on itself, with resentments enough to fill the couches of Vienna—yet beneath the surface there was faith, patience, and an implacable sense of destiny."[1] Chicago and Germany seem to be a natural pair—Chicago was one of the centers of German immigration in the nineteenth century, a migration that mirrored the complexity of nineteenth-century Germany itself. The German Catholics came and worked in the slaughterhouses. The German Protestants came and opened apothecary shops. The German Jews came to Chicago as merchants. There a hundred and fifty years ago they established the first Jewish congregation west of the Mississippi. German freethinkers and communists came and founded newspapers and laid the beginnings of the antislavery and union movements. All saw themselves as "Germans," as Bavarians or Rheinländer, as members of religious communities or actively free from such identity. Most saw themselves as engaging in the project of becoming Americans.

At the end of the millennium, Chicago remains a city of multiple ethnic heritages; only the Germans are missing. The legend has it that

the Germans are the best Americans because they most quickly assim-
ilated into American culture. What is left of German culture in Chicago
are the sad remnants of ethnicity—an Oktoberfest, often held in
September; the residue of a lost culture frozen in street names such as
Schiller and Goethe (pronounced Go-easy). A recent article in the
Chicago Tribune notes the "German flavor [that] lingers in Lincoln
Square." There the hundred-and-fifty-year-old homeopathic Merz
Apothecary with its "old-fashioned glass jars and dark wooden shelves
. . . [that] are so different from the typical Walgreens," is now owned by
Abdul Qaiyum, a Pakistani pharmacist. And it shares its "German"
space in Lincoln Square with the El Cheapo Grande Trading Post that
sells Native American artifacts and novelties.[2] On the same page a
much smaller article notes the quiet closing of the German restaurant
Zum Deutschen Eck (The German Corner), which had been a fixture on
Southport Avenue for fifty years. The very fragments of German identity in Chicago are still being transformed. The destruction of two
world wars, the horror of the Shoah, the Cold War, the absence of
major new influxes of German-speakers in the last fifty years have rendered any sense of a German ethnicity in all its complexity in Chicago
invisible. Neither the models of the melting pot nor those of multiculturalism grasp the reality of this fundamental shift in identity.

Given my work and my interests it is the German and the Jewish
aspects of Chicago that fascinate me. Recently, Ursula Hegi in her fascinating volume of interviews *Tearing the Silence* (1997) raised the question of the continuity of German (read: non-Jewish) experience in the
United States after the Shoah.[3] Hegi had gained mass popularity when
her Günther Grass–like novel *Stones from the River* (1994) was selected
as one of the first titles for Oprah Winfrey's TV book club. Young
Germans who, like Hegi, had come to the United States in their teens
in the 1960s and 1970s and were interviewed by her decades later, had
crafted an American identity around their guilt as Germans. Being
German was being responsible, was being historically marked. This
theme is also echoed in complex ways in Sabine Gölz's recent essay in
the *PMLA* special issue on ethnicity.[4] But what is striking about Hegi's

volume of carefully redrafted essays is the perpetuation of the dichotomy between Germans and Jews, one that haunts contemporary German writing on the topic, even when that writing is in English. Here I can mention the "philo-Semitic" autobiography by Björn Krondorfer, a young German-born historian now teaching in the United States, who also has written a participant-observer study of "the encounters between young Jews and Germans" (as per the subtitle of the volume).[5] The young Jews are American Jews on the East Coast. (As everyone knows, America is the Jewish country or at least New York is the Jewish city. Chicago is neither Jewish enough nor German enough in this fantasy landscape.) Germans are not Jews and Jews are not Germans. Yet it is in Chicago that the German-Jewish tradition of Reform Judaism still has its most powerful face. From Emil Hirsch to Arnold Wolf, from the founding of K.A.M.-Isaiah Israel, the first congregation west of the Mississippi, to the construction of Temple Sinai, its new building in the Near North dedicated in 1998, in Chicago there remains a strong German-Jewish presence. Yet American Reform Judaism, so very German in its conceptual foundation in the German Enlightenment and nineteenth-century German liberalism, rarely speaks of its German roots. With the acceptance of Zionism by the end of the 1940s and through the conceptual restructuring of Jewish identity by Shoah studies in the 1960s, American Reform Judaism carefully distanced itself from its German roots. English replaced German as the language of Jewish culture at the end of the nineteenth century. At the end of the twentieth century Hebrew dominates. Chicago's Reform Jews stopped being German Jews and became "Jews."

Fifty years ago the German Federal Republic was founded out of the ashes of the war and the horrors of the Shoah. What has remained in Chicago in the past fifty years is an invisible dichotomy between the world of a Jewish culture, greatly shaped by all of these earlier German experiences, and the invisible world of Germany and its cultural inheritance. Today, ten years after reunification and on the threshold of the founding of the Berlin Republic, Germany's presence in Chicago has begun to change. German ethnicity is again becoming a topic of interest and Jews, especially those of German heritage, can now begin to think of their complex origin as Jews and Germans. The guilt and anger articulated by the young German Americans interviewed by Hegi and the horror of young Jews about Germany is giving way to a sense of the complexity of a German ethnicity in Chicago. It is no longer embedded in the "German" places or tastes or language, but in the history of Germans and Jews. It is a shared history that is both a history of common goals and ideals and of horrors experienced and inflicted. It is a shared *history*. And in sharing that history a common moment in the present is being created. It is a sense of complexity that incorporates the tensions and memories of the past into a new and fruitful relationship.

The split between the Jewish and the German ideas of what it means to be a German in America is deep and yet is slowly being bridged. This split reflects a dichotomy underscored by the experience of National Socialism. However, it is this very dichotomy that is confronted by the desire to see a new Germany as part of a new Europe. For if the Germans, both Jews and non-Jews, in America came to be the best Americans because they so totally vanished into the "melting pot," the initial desire of postwar Germans (including the fragmentary presence of the Jewish community in Germany) after the Shoah was to become the "best Europeans." Moreover, in complex ways, they did. Now Europe is globalized as well as unified and that globalization, at least in the realms of culture, has a clearly German accent. The idea that culture is the central sphere in which Germans and Germany at home, in the new Europe, in a globalized economy, define themselves began to take shape fifty years ago here at the University of Chicago.

*

In June 1949, the faculty at the University of Chicago organized a conference to commemorate the bicentennial of the birth of the German poet-statesman, Johann Wolfgang von Goethe.[6] The renowned anti-Fascist Giuseppe Antonio Borgese, professor of Italian at the University of Chicago, exiled professor of German at the University of Milan, and the son-in-law of Thomas Mann, spearheaded the commemoration. He was enthusiastically joined in his efforts by Robert M. Hutchins, the president of the University of Chicago, then two decades into his project of restructuring American higher education, and Walter Paul Paepcke, head of the Container Corporation of America and a member of the University of Chicago board of directors. Held in Aspen, Colorado, the conference was the formative act of the famed Aspen Institute. It was also the moment in history when American intellectuals and politicians sought to bring a defeated and destroyed Germany back into the community of nations through the power of culture.

The missionary-physician-musician Albert Schweitzer, who was on his first and only trip to the United States, keynoted the conference, speaking first on the Hyde Park campus and then again in Aspen. He asked, "What is duty?" And he answered, "Goethe replied: 'What the day demands.' So too, it is for us to open our eyes, to realize our immediate duties, and to carry them out." This was the call to build a new world, and in it a new Germany, without the pall of ethnic and religious hatred. The Goethe bicentennial marked the moment following the Nazi horrors when the world learned that Goethe's ideal nation of culture would be the model for the new Federal Republic of Germany. Hutchins's call to this extraordinary event concluded:

> If man is somehow one and if the world is somehow one, it is not too soon to wonder what it is that unifies both man and world. World organization will be human community or it will not be at all. And the great society, fully, even distractedly, conscious of its divergences and distinctions, will not become the human community until it finds the common spirit that is man. We turn here to Goethe and search him, the better to turn to and search ourselves, and cry More Light! More Light!

"More light" was, as Karl Guthke has elegantly shown us, the putative last words heard by those gathered about Goethe on his deathbed.[7] An oddly appropriate phrase for the opening of a conference dedicated to the resurrection of German culture from its Nazi past. Fifty years later we stand at a point where the success of the Federal Republic as a democratic state is unquestioned. Yet we also stand at a new juncture in history. For it is now not the reconstitution of Germany but the creation of a new Germany, the Berlin Republic, in a newly united Europe that stands before us at the millennium. And that new Europe is clearly one driven by the German economic and cultural engine.

Now, 250 years after Goethe's birth, fifty years after the founding of the Federal Republic, and ten years after German reunification, Goethe's claim on our attention remains unquestioned. He complained on March 12, 1828, to Eckermann: "There is something more or less wrong among us old Europeans; our relations are far too artificial and complicated, our nutriment and mode of life are without their proper nature, and our social intercourse is without proper love and good will. Every one is polished and courteous; but no one has the courage to be hearty and true. . . ."[8] The charge to be true to the qualities demanded of the citizen of the nation-state has now become a clarion call to be both Germans and, as the Germans have strived so hard to be over the past fifty years, the best Europeans. Goethe's call was for a conversion of hidebound Europeans into universal human beings. And that was true especially among the intellectual elite of Germany: "Let us remain in a state of hopeful expectation as to the conditions of us Germans a century hence, and whether we shall then have advanced so far as to be no longer savants and philosophers, but human beings" (319). Our appropriation of Goethe's vision of his new Germany became the vision of the new Europe after World War II. The new Germany was to be understood in Goethe's terms. "I am not uneasy about the unity of Germany," said Goethe on October 23, 1828, "our good highways and future railroads will do their part. But, above all, may Germany be one in love! And may it always be one against the foreign foe! May it be one, so that the German dollar and groschen may be of equal value throughout the Empire! One so that my suitcases can pass unopened through all the thirty-six states! May it be one, so that the passport of a citizen of Weimar may not be considered insufficient . . . by the frontier guard of a neighboring state! . . . May Germany be one in weight and measure, in trade and commerce, and a hundred similar things which I will not name!" (350). And it is in the realm of culture, of the "quantity of the German theaters" that Goethe pointed to admiringly, that he saw the central force that could link the nation.

*

At the beginning of a new century that nation called Germany is now the new "Berlin Republic." The capital of the Federal Republic of Germany has now "returned to Berlin." (As it had "returned" in the 1920s during the Weimar Republic, so-called because the constitution was hammered out in the National Theater in Weimar. As it had "returned" in 1949 when the city became the capital of the German Democratic Republic.) It is a Berlin that struggles for an identity. Identity, both individual and collective, is what Paul Gilroy has called "a changing same."[9] Is it the old imperial Berlin? The desire to rebuild the old Imperial Palace on what was in the GDR the Marx-Engels-Platz led in the mid-1980s to the erection of a full size mock-facade painting of the palace in front of the old GDR Parliament building. With the Imperial Palace's virtual recreation all of the twentieth century could vanish into an imagined Berlin Republic whose lineage would trace without interruption to imperial Germany.

Or was it the world of the Weimar Republic that should serve as the model? In April 1990, Ulrich Eckardt, the long-term director of the Berlin Festival, called a news conference. He announced that out of the long-existing cultural competition between the island city of "Westberlin" and (East) Berlin, the "capital of the German Democratic Republic," a new "European cultural metropolis would arise": "We stand at a new moment in Berlin, which, from the standpoint of resources and historical echoes, is very similar to the period before 1933; we stand in close proximity to the cultural palette of the 1920s with its mixing of Western and Eastern influences" [*Frankfurter Rundschau* (April 6, 1990): 2]. The headline above the Eckardt news conference story that morning in the *TAZ*, Berlin's popular liberal daily, read: "Berlin Dreams the Dream of the Twenties" [*Die Tageszeitung*

(Berlin) (April 6, 1990): 1]. This prophecy of the cultural rebirth of Weimar Berlin came six months after the fall of the Wall, three months before German economic union (on July 1, 1990), and six months before the absorption of the German Democratic Republic (GDR) into the Federal Republic of Germany (FRG). At that moment, the promise of the newly reunited city could be best expressed through a direct evocation of what seemed to its cultural leaders its most memorable past.

The counterimage to such a vision of Weimar Berlin as a cultural ideal was put forth two years later in the aftermath of innumerable incidents of racially motivated murders, beatings, and arson carried out by a relatively small number of right-wing hatemongers in areas all across Germany during 1992. The young Social Democratic politician Wolfgang Thierse, later to become president of the German Parliament under the Social Democratic/Green coalition of 1998, commented: "What has happened in the past months in the freshly reunited Germany reminds one—I cannot and will not resist this comparison— of horrible images from the final days of the Weimar Republic and fascist Germany: the broken windows in the dormitories of those seeking political asylum; the ransacked shops of Jewish neighbors during the pogrom-night of November 9, 1938; the marches of threatening skinheads and 'fachos'; the SA marches with their shouts of 'sieg heil'; the hunt for foreigners in the subways; the hunt for Jews in the cities of 'Greater Germany'" [*Berliner Morgenpost* (August 30, 1992): 1]. Here, Thierse presented a compelling vision of Berlin as the city in which the collapse of Weimer democracy could be charted most clearly.

Is it possible to imagine another model for the Berlin Republic— that of Goethean universality coupled with a late-twentieth-century particularism? Neither the Weimar Germany of Goethe, nor that of Rathenau, and certainly not the Reich of Wilhelm II, nor that of Hitler can serve as the model for this new German state. Yet all are present in its ancestry. But in the struggles about what defines the new Berlin Republic there remains that central question, "Who is a German?" It is this question that lies at the heart of the recent revitalization of the moribund German cultural scene of the 1980s. It is this question that links the pressing concerns of East-West identity formation with the broader issues of national, ethic, and religious identity. Can the American model of multiculturalism be in harmony with the striving to bridge the extraordinary differences in experience and expectation of all of the inhabitants of the "New Lands" (the former GDR) and the "Old Lands" (the now "successful" Federal Republic)?[10] What can replace the collapsed, Cold War model that saw Berlin (and thus Germany) as the site of confrontation, both political (as in the Berlin airlift and the shootings at the Wall) as well as cultural? The city's identity through the 1980s was a Cold War identity and this drove the rich, cultural life of both halves of the divided Berlin. How is the new Berlin Republic to be distinct from this world?

If this new idea of the Berlin Republic would be a continuation of the imagined world of Imperial or Weimar Germany, where is the ethical confrontation with the Nazi or the GDR past? Are ethics the central problem as old systems both in the East and the West confront the new Berlin Republic? Is the xenophobia felt toward Vietnamese cigarette sellers (remnants of the old GDR) in any way parallel to the sense of disappointment and anger felt toward those political leaders, such as Helmut Kohl and Wolfgang Schäubele, who formed the united Germany and who have now been charged with corruption? Need one speak of ethics when we examine the goals and structures of the Berlin Republic?

German history in the twentieth century, more than the history of any other nation, demands of its citizens an ethical account of its present and its future world. From World War I, according to the argument made by Fritz Fischer, through the cannibalization of Czechoslovakia, Poland, Russia, and much of Western and Northern Europe, up to and including the Shoah, ethical conduct was not the hallmark of the German state.[11] Indeed, unethical conduct was widespread well beyond the realm of individual political leaders and institutions, a painful realization Germany is still coming to terms with. The hotly contested photographic exhibit organized by Hannes Heer and others at the Hamburg Institute for Social Research in 1995, for instance, represented the barbaric actions of the German army (the *Wehrmacht*) in World War II. The exhibit focused on the actions of the "common soldier," the little man and his role in the murder of Europe's Jews. That the debate about this issue, like the debate around the planned Peter Eisenman–designed Memorial to the Murdered Jews of Europe in Berlin, does not seem to end, is a clear sign of the ethical obsessiveness of German society with its Nazi past.

The new Germany is not only concerned with what is right and wrong but, more centrally, how to tell stories about past events so that the moral ground is kept visible. In his book *The Gift of Death*, Jacques Derrida notes that "the narrative is genealogical but it is not simply an act of memory. It bears witness, in the manner of an ethical or political act, for today and for tomorrow. It means first of all thinking about what takes place today."[12] From Goethe's Buchenwald to Hitler's Buchenwald to 1999, the year that Weimar (and, by extension, Buchenwald) was the European cultural capital, this ethical focus has not abated. In 1999, the city of Weimar presented an exhibit called "From the Face to the Mask: Vienna-Weimar-Buchenwald 1939" in the Goethe House. There visitors saw the life masks and death masks of men and women who had been racial and political prisoners of the Third Reich and whose visages had been captured for the delectation of racial anthropologists. In Buchenwald there were displayed copies of furniture made by inmates of the concentration camp, copies of the furniture in the Goethe House. All of this in the former GDR, in the "New States," in the older Thuringia, now new again.

The new Germany with its self-consciously ethical confrontations with the past, at least the past of the Shoah and the Nazis, seemed to be no less acutely desirous of an ethical dealing with the immediate past, at least the GDR past. In searching for those who were "corrupted" by the Communist system of the GDR, everyone was suspect, if not presumptively guilty (like the characters in G. K. Chesterton's *The Man who was Thursday*, where all of the members of an anarchist group turn out to be police informers). All of the early political leaders from the GDR, from Christa Wolf (who was spoken about in 1990 as a candidate for president of the GDR) down to the only leader from that now so-damned past still active, Manfred Stolpe, the Social Democratic prime minister of Brandenburg; from the cultural establishment (Hermann Kant) to the cultural avant-garde (Sascha Anderson) to the cultural opposition (again Christa Wolf), all were involved to one degree or another. Only those expelled or jailed (such as Wolf Biermann, Erich Loehst, Walter Janka, and Robert Havemann), those who could claim their ethical position from beyond the Wall or from within the walls of prison or imposed internal exile could comfortably wear the mantle of innocence. Moreover, many of these refused to feel themselves superior, knowing the totality of a system powerful enough to even periodically permit types of internal dissidence.

In today's Berlin Republic it is not the state corruption of the GDR that defines the ethical. The new ethics revolve about the old Federal Republic and the "duty" (the word oft spoken by Helmut Kohl in the winter of 1999–2000) of the members of the Christian Democratic Union that, as the self-proclaimed sole uncorrupted, democratic party in Germany, crafted reunification virtually single-handedly. ("Duty" is a damaged word out of the now distant and memorialized German past. It was the explanation for actions taken during World War II and the Shoah. "I was just doing my duty," was a constant refrain.) The Social Democrats, certainly after the fall of Willy Brandt in 1974 over the Günter Guillaume affair (when a top-level spy from the GDR was revealed to have a senior position on his staff), were seen by the Christian Democrats as "fellow travelers." The Communists, banned in the Federal Republic since the late 1960s, were clearly the enemy. Only the truth of the Christian Democratic Union could maintain the bulwark of anticommunism. Ethical violations of existing laws concerning campaign contributions (or were they political bribes?) were a lesser evil than the "evil empire."

The ethics of explaining these actions fell in complicated ways into a half-remembering of that damaged past. When Casimir Prinz zu Sayn-Wittgenstein, the treasurer of the Christian Democratic Union in Hesse, sought to explain the existence of a foreign bank account numbering in the millions of marks, he invented "Jewish citizens who passed away and wanted to show their appreciation for the old city of Frankfurt" and thus left their fortunes in Swiss banks to the party and to the state.[13] Henryk Broder, the German-Jewish essayist whose voice is heard elsewhere in this volume, was right when he wrote decades ago, concerning the great popularity in West Germany of the aging and ill German-Jewish exile writer Erich Fried, that "Germans love dead and half-dead Jews." The ethics of memory come to be reshaped by the necessity of the present in the light of the stereotypes of the past. Harald Martenstein, writing in *Der Tagesspiegel* about the Hessian affair, concluded his commentary with an ironic fantasy of what the culture of the Berlin Republic could also become. He imagines the Christian Democratic Union creating a literary prize for which German writers would "narrate the lives of Moshe Silberberg and Sarah Goldstein and all of the other ghosts, who at the end of their earthly lives still wanted to become good Germans."[14] The German stories that frame the ethical dilemmas of the present are often cast in the fantasies of the past. So why not make acceptable cultural objects—novels, plays, and tales—out of them? Here the tension is between the craft of the poet, whose "lying" frames the world (pace Oscar Wilde), and the duplicity of the politician, whose lying falls into historical obfuscation.

Such fantasies occur at the end of history as Francis Fukuyama quite correctly noted about 1989. In the Berlin Republic they also mirror the beginning of history, the moment of the creation of the two German states in 1949.[15] The ethical problems of speaking in another's voice are as central to the rethinking of the Berlin Republic as they were to the rethinking of the Third Reich when in 1948 the famed novelist of the "small form" Wolfgang Koeppen sat down and wrote the "autobiography" of a survivor of the Shoah, Jakob Littner, now understood as Koeppen's first novel.[16] Can there be only one "German" voice, one voice that subsumes the GDR, that subsumes the ethnic and classes discourses of "Germany" into a single German voice? And must that German voice speak "German"?

Many of the ethnically diverse voices in Germany, from the

Turkish-German writer Emine Sevgi Özdamar to the Rumanian-German writer Hertha Müller to the German-Brazilian writer Zé do Rock, wrestled with the ethical question of what could constitute the appropriate German voice for the new Berlin Republic well before its creation. Today they too struggle with the ghosts of the past as embedded in the idea of what defines the German. Is it the meaning of language, the idea of a particular history, or the borders that each of them crossed to come to Germany that motivates them most? In their presence in the culture of the new Berlin Republic a new turn can be felt. It is the voice of those who have already crossed a border into the new Germany.

Border crossing remains the central metaphor for the culture of the new Berlin Republic. At the end of Emine Sevgi Özdamar's great novel of the Turkish experience, *Das Leben ist eine Karawanserei*, her protagonist is on a train from Istanbul to Germany. Hertha Müller's first works published in the Federal Republic record her protagonist's transition from the German-speaking village in Rumania where she was raised to a new life in Germany. Zé do Rock's first book (an autobiography cast as a novel) is a comic account of his protagonist's travels around Germany and the world as a young Brazilian.[17] This focus on the crossing of borders is also seen in *Sohara's Trip* (1996), the most recent novel by Barbara Honigmann. This account of the search for the kidnapped children of a North African Jewish woman has its protagonist crossing borders aided by a German-Jewish exile in France. Honigmann herself was born in East Berlin in 1949, the daughter of German Jews who returned to "build Socialism." She left the GDR in 1984 for Strasbourg in order to live an orthodox Jewish life, a life that would have been conceptually as well as practically impossible for her in either East or West Germany. All of these writers mark the new Germany and its potential by the borders crossed, by the notion of a transition into a new, if complicated future.

And what is one to do with those American Jews such as Jeanette Lander and Irene Dische who have crossed linguistic as well as political borders to become German writers? The borders they have crossed are cultural as well as linguistic. In her novels Jeanette Lander reworks the German language in her accounts of the American-Jewish and the German-Jewish past, the crossing of borders because of exile and acculturation. Irene Dische relies on translators to bring her English-language tales about Germans in America and Americans in Germany into German, but is read in Germany as a German-Jewish writer. The borders crossed are complex and contradictory.

The major younger writers of the former GDR also focus on the crossing of borders, their hopes for elimination, and their odd retention as part of the mentality of the new Germany. Ingo Schulze, in his *Simple Stories: Tales from the East-German Provinces* (1998), the best fictional account of the transition from the closed and armed borders to the GDR to the new Berlin Republic, begins his novel with a first trip from the crumbling GDR to Italy in February 1990.[18] The "Wall in the Head," the sense of distance between East and West, is a psychological quality of the culture of the Berlin Republic, not only between East and West but among the various voices heard from every corner of the new republic. It is the thematization of these qualities of difference that defines and will continue to define the culture of the Berlin Republic.

The evolution of the Berlin Republic has already begun. It is not merely the rebuilding of Berlin, not solely the movement of the capital from the Rhine to the Spree, but the unraveling of the beliefs of the Cold War and the constitution of a new mentality captured in a new cultural world. It is the de facto recognition that Germany is a land of many voices and many cultures—of Turks who have become Germans; of Russian Jews who have become Germans; of "Ostlers" who have become Germans; and of "Westlers" who are becoming, like all the others, citizens of the new Germany. It is the growing awareness that the past in all of its variety needs to be understood and often confronted. Multiculturalism in this Germany means the reestablishment of regionalism in the "New States." Saxon again replaces Bavarian as the standard "comic" accent and the isolation of Saarbrüken or Flensburg must now be reconsidered when one thinks of Rostock and Schwerin.

In the new Europe, the Euro is replacing the deutsche mark, an event as disturbing, if not more disturbing, to those who became

German first through the currency reform of 1990, when getting "real" marks defined the first step toward a new German identity.[19] The initial desire was to join the world in which, according to a thirteen-year-old in Thuringia in 1991, the marmalade and the chocolate tasted better.[20] But the desire for reunification on the level of acculturation gave way in the course of the 1990s to "Ostalgia," nostalgia for the sense of community as well as the tastes and forms of the now mythologized GDR. The world lost when the border is crossed is also the world of the "non-Germans" in the Berlin Republic.

For those marginalized in society, living in dormitories in the German cities set aside for those seeking exile or in city districts dominated by "foreigners" (many of whom were born and raised there), money too defined their Germanness. It was the economic forces of the economic miracle that brought them to Germany and kept them there. It was the openness of a German society that enabled they to live there. In addition, it is this same openness that permits them to slowly but certainly become part of the Culture (writ large) of that society. As the children of the displaced persons after 1945 became the good German Jews of the 1970s and 1980s, so too the Turkish Germans and Arab Germans and Afro-Germans have become a new presence in the mass and high culture of the Berlin Republic. Like the Jews, this multicultural addition to German society comes from the New as well as the Old Lands. In *The Black Atlantic*, Paul Gilroy speaks of such identities as "located in the shift between the oral and the written culture" (219), as well as "lodged between the local and the global" (9). In this tension between oppositions, identity cannot be understood as "a fixed essence nor as a vague and utterly contingent construction to be reinvented by the whim and will of aesthetics, symbolism, and language gamers" (102). In the Berlin Republic these groups truly bring their own cultural traditions with them, whether as the children of African-American service men or of Namibian freedom fighters. Now all are new Germans in the new Europe. They inhabit what Lavie and Swedenburg have labeled as a "third time-space" that is located between the idea of "identity as essence" and "identity as conjecture."[21] Such a space, the new Germany in the new Europe, can be multiply "hyphenated," as a punctuation mark that simultaneously connects and separates forms of identity.

*

Thus the question of the German American and his/her vanished place in the multicultural landscape can serve as a model and a warning for the Berlin Republic. In the twentieth century Germans became the best Americans; they were transformed into other categories, losing their "German" identity. In the fifty years after the end of World War II West Germans and East Germans became the best Europeans. The West Germans subsumed themselves into a unified Europe defined by the European Union and NATO; the East Germans into a Communist world defined by the Warsaw Pact and the Comintern. Over the first ten years of reunification, these two halves, now united, have struggled with what the new German identity is to be defined by in the course of reconstituting a new Central Europe. In becoming Americans through the pressures of both world wars, Germans vanished into the world of America. German Jews became "Jews." Other Germans simply became "Americans." Recently, as Ursula Hegi has shown, there is a growing discomfort with this invisibility. A new German-American sensibility is growing. It can be seen on the part of German-American academics such as Werner Sollors at Harvard University and Frank Trommler at the University of Pennsylvania, who have now taken to redefining the German-American tradition from the seventeenth century through the present with a great sense of inclusion. So, for them the German Jews of the nineteenth and twentieth century are again "Germans." The Germans are becoming reinscribed into the sense of an American history that defines the American present. They are now there in the past and, therefore, in complex ways, also in the present.

In becoming citizens of the Berlin Republic and thus of a Germany enmeshed in the cultural transformations of the new Europe, this process of acculturation and assimilation will also take place. But as German attitudes, values, and voices remain contested within the new Germany of the Berlin Republic, this can be a fruitful process. German cultural life will continue to be transformed and become ever more interesting. The centripetal forces of regionalism, multiculturalism, and linguistic diversity will continue to shape those centrifugal forces that continue to define Germany by land, language, and blood. It is in these tensions that cultural form takes place, as it did in the years from 1945 to 1949, when a new German culture evolved in both Germanys. Once again the German cultural landscape finds itself in the process of widespread transformation.

In the light of these changes, the Department of Germanic Studies at the University of Chicago organized an exploration into some of those questions that now confront a united Germany in a united Europe. Keynoted by the former president of the Federal Republic of Germany, Richard von Weizsäcker, the conference framed the contemporary state of German self-awareness. Of all of the leaders of the Federal Republic of Germany, it was von Weizsäcker who called for the moral leadership of Germany in the light of the German past, in the light of the Shoah, as well as in the light of a new German future in Europe. President of Germany at the moment of reunification, he showed the moral leadership that made it possible to conceive of such a political act as not the aggressive culmination of victory in a cultural battle but as the first step toward realizing the dream of a new and different nation. Now we step back and regard this moment—in which a quarter of a millennium has passed since Goethe was born, fifty years have gone by since the founding of the Federal Republic of Germany and the German Democratic Republic, and ten years have elapsed since German reunification. What can the new Germany look like as the center of the new Europe, a Europe without boundaries and border guards, with a common currency, with a new globalized culture? Or, to phrase it as a question such as that which confronted the listeners in 1949 at the Goethe bicentennial in Aspen: Can Goethe's ideals of an international culture be the guideposts for Germany's sense of self for the next half-century?

In this volume, we examine the relationship between existing political culture in today's Germany and the cultural ideals of a new Europe. And we do so specifically in the light of the lessons learned from German unification and European union. Leading German-based cultural and political figures have been paired with American-based academic figures to address these crucial questions from a variety of perspectives. The German-based authors form a core of the intellectual elite of the Berlin Republic. Barbara John, the secretary for foreigners of the senate of Berlin, reflects on the future of a new multicultural Germany in the new Europe; Peter Schneider, who ranks among Germany's preeminent novelists, addresses the future of German and European cultures and languages in a unified Europe; Henryk Broder, columnist and correspondent of *Der Spiegel*, turns his attention to the diversification of the cultural marketplace; Monika Treut, one of German cinema's most consistently interesting and provocative figures, looks at the diminishing role of German cinema in international film culture; and Tom Freudenheim, a German-Jewish American who is the deputy director of the Jewish Museum in Berlin, investigates the process of memory and memorialization in the new Europe.

The Chicago participants with whom these writers are paired are equally well-suited to comment on the new Berlin Republic's future from a transatlantic perspective. Saskia Sassen, a Dutch-born and Italian- and American-educated professor of sociology at the University of Chicago, takes up the topic of transnationalism within and beyond the realm of immigration policy; Helmut Müller-Sievers, a German American who serves as head of the Kaplan Center for the Humanities at Northwestern University, examines the centrality of the figures of Goethe and Humboldt in the German conception of itself as a homogenous nation; Dagmar Lorenz, a German American who is the author of the definitive study of German-Jewish women writers and serves as professor of German at the University of Illinois–Chicago, looks at postunification German literature; David Levin, the son of German-Jewish immigrants and associate professor of Germanic and cinema and media studies at the University of Chicago, provides a study of Monika Treut's films that is at once retrospective and prospective and addresses larger questions about the role of the Newer German Cinema; Howard Sulkin, president of the Spertus Institute, an institution of Jewish higher education in Chicago, examines the difficult and uncertain work that museums can and must do at the beginning of a new millennium; and Andreas Glaeser, a German-American assistant professor of sociology at the University of Chicago, addresses the topic of memory, memorialization, and urban planning in the old-new, East-West city of Berlin.

The conference which was the origin for these papers took place at the University of Chicago on June 9–10, 1999, and was sponsored by the German American Marshall Fund, the German Academic Exchange Service, the Philip and Ida Romberg Fund for German American Relations of the Department of Germanic Studies of the University of Chicago, and the Franke Institute for the Humanities of the University of Chicago. It was organized by Sander L. Gilman, the Henry R. Luce Distinguished Service Professor of the Liberal Arts in Human Biology at the University of Chicago, and Todd Herzog, of the Department of Germanic Studies there, with the assistance of Hillary Hope Herzog, Sharlyn Rhee, James Cantranella, Anke Pinkert, and Ashley Passmore. The *spiritus rector* of this event was the German counsel-general in Chicago, Michael Engelhard. A true polymath, translator of Michelangelo and Pushkin, and a major collector of Goethena, Michael Engelhard helped to focus and frame this conference. He was helpful without ever seeking to push; he was encouraging without ever being demanding. It is to him that this volume is dedicated.

Sander L. Gilman
Chicago
Friday, January 21, 2000

NOTES

1. *The New York Times*, 25 May 1999, B6.

2. *The Chicago Tribune*, 23 January 2000, 5:1.

3. Ursula Hegi, *Tearing the Silence: On Being German in America* (New York: Simon and Schuster, 1997).

4. Sabine Gölz, "How Ethnic Am I?" *PMLA* 113 (1998): 46–51.

5. Björn Krondorfer, *Remembrance and Reconciliation: Encounters Between Young Jews and Germans* (New Haven, CT: Yale University Press, 1995).

6. I am indebted for the material on the first Goethe conference to the work of Sidney Hyman, *The Aspen Idea* (Norman: University of Oklahoma Press, 1975).

7. Karl S. Guthke, *Last Words: Variations on a Theme in Cultural History* (Princeton, NJ: Princeton University Press, 1992).

8. Johann Wolfgang von Goethe, *Conversations of Goethe: with Eckermann and Soret*, trans. John Oxenford (London : G. Bell & Sons, 1879), 315.

9. Paul Gilroy, *The Black Atlantic: Modernity and Double Consciousness* (Cambridge, MA: Harvard University Press, 1996), 101.

10. On the problems of public ethics at times of historical and cultural shifts see Dennis F. Thompson, "Mediated Corruption: The Case of the Keating Five," *American Polical Science Review* 87 (1993): 369–81.

11. Fritz Fischer, *Krieg der Illusionen: Die deutsche Politik von 1911 bis 1914* (Düsseldorf: Droste, 1970).

12. Jacques Derrida, *The Gift of Death*, trans. David Wills (Chicago: University of Chicago Press), 35.

13. Roger Cohen, "Kohl Resigns German Party Post after He Is Rebuked for Scandal," *The New York Times*, 19 January 2000, A10.

14. Harald Martenstein, "Ihr letzter Wille," *Der Tagesspiegel,* 18 January 2000, 2.

15. Francis Fukuyama, *The End of History and the Last Man* (New York: Avon Books, 1992). See also Howard Williams, *Francis Fukuyama and the End of History* (Cardiff: University of Wales Press, 1997).

16. Wolfgang Koeppen, *Jakob Littners Aufzeichnungen aus einem Erdloch* (Frankfurt: Jüdischer Verlag, 1992).

17. Emine Sevgi Özdamar, *Das Leben ist eine Karawanserei hat zwei Türen aus Einer Kam ich Rein aus der Anderen Ging ich Raus* (Cologne: Kiepenheuer & Witsch paperback, 1992); Herta Müller, *Reisende auf einem Bein* (Hamburg: Rowohlt paperback, 1989); Zé do Rock, *fom winde ferfeelt* (Munich: diá, 1995).

18. Ingo Schulze, *Simple Stories: Ein Roman aus der ostdeutschen Provinz* (Berlin: Berlin Verlag, 1998). Translated by John E. Woods as *Simple Stories* (New York: Knopf, 2000).

19. Konrad H. Jarausch, *Die unverhoffte Einheit 1989-1990* (Frankfurt: Suhrkamp, 1995), 214–20.

20. Regina Rusch, ed., *Plötzlich ist alles ganz anders: Kinder schreiben über unser Land* (Frankfurt: Eichborn, 1992), 13–14.

21. Smadar Lavie and Ted Swedenburg, "Introduction" to their edited volume *Displacement, Diaspora, and Geographies of Identity* (Durham, NC: Duke University Press, 1996), 1–25, here 17.

CAN GOETHE GUIDE US
THROUGH THE PROCESS
OF EUROPEAN UNION?

Richard von Weizsäcker

I.

In an act of outstanding magnanimity and farsighted confidence President Robert Maynard Hutchins and faculty members at the University of Chicago assembled a conference in 1949 on the occasion of Goethe's two hundredth birthday. Among the main topics under discussion was the question of whether Goethe's ideals of an international culture could become once again the guideposts for Germany's future.

Goethe's 1949 bicentennial coincided with the foundation of the Federal Republic of Germany. But in 1949 the German Democratic Republic also came into being, as a puppet state of the Soviet Union. The division of Germany was thus sealed for more than forty years. This deep split, with all its human suffering, was, in the first place, a result of recent German history. We, the Germans, had waged aggressive wars with practically all of our neighboring countries. At the end of World War II and as an immediate consequence of the indescribable crimes and brutal atrocities committed by Hitler's Germany, there was no legitimized German state authority between 1945 and 1949. These crimes had been committed in the name of an ideology claiming the role of a so-called *Herrenvolk* for a so-called German race, with the aim of subjugating or annihilating others, in particular the Jews.

Further back in history Germany had been the cradle of Communism. Marx and Engels were Germans. Undoubtedly they were far from anticipating any of the ruining harm brought about by the ideology that had been produced out of their thoughts. But those ideologies did bring untold misery upon hundreds of millions of human beings. The Stalinist Soviet Union was a real and immediate threat to world peace and to the survival of free democracies. It was no mere coincidence that NATO had been founded in the same year as the Federal Republic of Germany. At that time, Western Germany was the easternmost outpost of the Western world. The border between the two blocs went right across our country. It became clear rather quickly that to protect freedom and democracy West Germany must be integrated into the defense system of the West. Yet it took courage and confidence to accomplish this. The Federal Republic of Germany was firmly based on a democratic constitution, but one with little democratic tradition behind it. The Weimar Republic had failed after fourteen years under the steadily growing pressure of antidemocratic groups, both on the extreme left and right. Poverty, unemployment, and an isolated foreign policy situation added up to domestic fights that could almost be characterized as a civil war and ended with Hitler's dictatorship.

A living democracy cannot flourish on institutions alone. It must rise out of the spirit of its people. For the American nation it had been decisive that its basic founding principles and its constitution had been formulated by some of the greatest and deepest minds of modern political times. The largest part of a German democratic elite had been forced into emigration or was murdered after the anti-Hitler plot of July 20, 1944. After the war, the best among the survivors got together to work out a new constitution. They represented trustworthy traditions of the German mind and drew the necessary conclusions from the wrongs in German history. Their achievement was the constitution of the Federal Republic of Germany, which, throughout the second half of our century, proved to be a solid basis for a reliable German democracy. Nevertheless, in 1949 the world still looked upon Germany with mistrust—all too understandable in view of frightening recent experiences. While America, pursuing a most generous policy, included

Germany in the Marshall Plan and saved the population of West Berlin from the Soviet blockade, there were still deep-seated international misgivings as to the course Germany would take in the future. This is what led the first British general secretary of NATO to offer his notorious explanation of why West Germany should be invited to join NATO: to keep the Russians out, the Americans in, and the Germans down. But this was by no means the only and final answer of the Western democracies. They looked deeply into German culture in order to find the substance out of which a new democratic, freedom-loving, and humane future of Germany could grow. Time and again, it was one name they rediscovered and put their confidence in: Johann Wolfgang von Goethe.

It was in the same year of 1949 that UNESCO produced a special volume in honor of Goethe. In this publication the most prominent and learned representatives of European, American, Asian, and African culture rendered their respect for Goethe's humanity. It was out of the same sense of respect that the world-famous Aspen Institute was founded under the auspices of Goethe and in a celebration of his bicentennial. Giuseppe Antonio Borghese, University of Chicago President Robert M. Hutchins, and Walter-Paul Paepcke, University of Chicago board member and chairman of the Container Corporation of America, were the leaders of this initiative.

II.

Why did Goethe's ideals fascinate the world at that time? There is, I think, a simple answer to this question: obviously, the spirit of Goethe was a spirit of peace. This was a man utterly unable to hate other peoples. After the campaign against Napoleon, Germans reproached Goethe for having contributed no war songs against the French. His answer: it would have been necessary to hate the French in order to compose war poetry. "But how could I have hated a nation which is among the most cultivated on earth and to whom I owe such a large part of my own formation?" In his view, any nationalism was simply stupid, in particular a German nationalism: "On the lowest level of culture you will find national hatred at its strongest and most pugnacious degree. However, there is a level where it disappears altogether, where you find yourself beyond nations and where you sense good or evil of a neighbor as if it were yours. This level was in accordance with my nature."

And therefore he also was a convinced European. He always encouraged newly reemerging European cultures, especially those of Eastern and Southeastern Europe, such as Czech, Polish, Serbian, and Russian, by pointing to the dignity and beauty of their poetry and their spiritual traditions. Nowhere has this Europeanism of Goethe produced a greater impact than in France, a country that customarily encounters Germany with mixed feelings, ranging from reserve and skepticism to dislike and hatred. But French confidence in Goethe's spirit never waned. In 1932 André Suares wrote a book with the title *Goethe—le Grand Européen*. "Europe," Suares remarked, "is an empty notion without Goethe." And, according to Henri Lichtenberger, Goethe was "the good, the greatest European, possibly the sublimist type of wisdom on the world." Paul Valéry considered Goethe "by worldwide approval promoted to the highest ranking, among the fathers of thought and graduation, of poetry: *Pater aestheticus in aeternum*." Romain Rolland commented that "Goethe is the poet who never lied." Finally, André Gide added, "This genius, to whom I owe undoubtedly more than to anyone else, perhaps more than to all of them put together." Those great Frenchmen wanted to establish how Goethe offered a hope against the historical mistakes of his people, how his spirit unites peoples, instead of separating them.

And Goethe's mind transcended even Europe. He had learned from Herder that every culture in the world deserved equal dignity. Goethe appreciated Chinese and Japanese culture just as much as he venerated Persian and Arabic culture. He also took the most lively interest in the beginnings of America's own literature:

> *Laßt alle Völker unter gleichem Himmel*
> *sich dieser Gabe wohlgemut erfreuen.*

Let all peoples under the same heavens
enjoy this joyous gift.

It was this respect that led him to his notion of *Weltliteratur* (world literature). It may sound presumptuous, but I don't think it really is, to rediscover this thought in the idea of UNESCO. *Weltliteratur*, as understood by Goethe, was both a fact and a challenge. By his deep attention, he learned to understand how the human spirit is at home everywhere. At the same time he sensed the increase, and growing danger, of nationalism. That is why he wanted to establish a universal principle, appealing to every culture never to put itself above any other culture, but rather to include itself into the entire *Weltkultur* (world culture), and to honor and to venerate the good wherever it was to be found.

III.

In our time, even more than in Goethe's, this attitude is a precondition for peace. Thanks to our communication technology we are in constant touch with people in every corner of the world. No longer can we afford not to care about faraway cultures. If I speak on the phone to someone from Japan, Zimbabwe, or Bolivia without caring about his or her way of thinking about the world, which is tantamount to imposing my German culture as the one that matters, I will produce another little wedge between cultures. And billions of such little wedges can lead to deep splits between peoples, when instead we need to be brought closer together.

Both in Germany and in America, there are reasons for concern, however, that cultures are tending to drift apart from one another. For instance, there seems to be a declining willingness to learn foreign languages. How, then, is this global village of communication to succeed? How are we to preserve peace if a growing number of peoples refuse to understand the languages of the others?

In a sometimes superficial way there are Europeans who demonstrate uneasiness about a loss of a European self-identity and a menacing American cultural dominance. In this context they prefer to speak about "soft culture." They point to intellectual fast food like *Reader's Digest*. They are afraid of a consumer culture, seeing it as a modification of Descartes: "Je pense?—non—Je consume, donc *je* suis." A French writer recently published a rather thoughtful book, *Retour a Berlin*, in which she uttered a deep sigh in Germany's direction: "If only you Germans would be a bit more self-confident culturally, you would not need to annoy us, the French, by being so German economically."

Personally, I have to admit an unpleasant incident in my own family. Three decades ago our youngest son, at the age of eight, had collected more Mickey Mouse comic strips than my wife felt was appropriate. After being gently reproached, he hid them away on a bookshelf. One day, when he returned from school, he found out, much to his alarm, that his cunning device had been discovered. Yet he did not give in. With a furious voice he presented his treasure to his mother and said: "My Mickey Mouse is to me what your Goethe is to you." Many years later, however, he belonged to those who could profit immensely from American culture and science at one of your outstanding universities. In my own family, we obviously had neglected Goethe's advice when he strongly recommended books to enable children to become aware as early as possible of the merits of other nations.

IV.

Every culture is indebted to others. The postwar German democratic culture received its most important impulses from the United States in every field of human activity—in politics and economics, in literature and music, in the way we speak, dress and sometimes—*horribile dictu*—even eat. More important of course are our common roots, deriving from the Enlightenment, our philosophical and ethical identity, consisting of tolerance and self-confidence. The Americans were the first to draw the necessary political conclusions for the rule of law, democracy, and human rights. And twice in our century they engaged themselves to fight with their lives for those principles and for the rescue of freedom in Europe.

There has never been a one-way traffic across the Atlantic. Americans as well have received much from Europe, including Germany and particularly Goethe. Ralph Waldo Emerson and his friends lived in Concord, which in its impact for American culture may be comparable to Weimar for German culture. It was Emerson's endeavor to put the United States culturally on its own feet. And these efforts went on to quite an extent in relation to Goethe. Emerson himself, Henry David Thoreau, and Margret Fuller passionately discussed Goethe's works.

This mutual process is still under way. Recently two American authors have written what are by far the two most important new books on Goethe. One of them digs deeply into the archives to investigate dark spots in Goethe's character. The other one, a tremendous biography, puts Goethe in the center of his and our times.

Emerson and Longfellow put Goethe in the same line as Benjamin Franklin. Others have proposed a comparison between Goethe and Thomas Jefferson. In fact the architecture of the University of Virginia in Charlottesville may be the most perfect realization of what Goethe, in his time, was dreaming of in terms of a humane concept of architecture. It is an expression of a spirit of freedom void of any dogmatism, including the dogmatism of churches. And is it mere chance that just this university was the first in the United States to teach German language, literature, and philosophy? A deeper knowledge of the exchange between the American and the European spirit—relations with Germany are but one aspect of American relations with Europe— could help both sides substantially, I believe, to come to an understanding of themselves. At the beginning of a new century and a new millennium it is appropriate to be conscious of what we share and where we differ, in order to cultivate what we have in common and to respect the differences.

V.

Let me propose a look both backward and forward at Europe in a more general historical and political perspective. With the devastating Thirty Years' War in the seventeenth century, the era of religious warfare in Europe came to an end. France came out on top. In the center of the continent there was hardly anything left but a political vacuum provoking new menaces and temptations. After another century, enlightenment successfully undermined the ancien régime. Emerging out of the French Revolution, Napoleon initiated the first attempt to bring about by force a modern type of European unification. Intellectuals like La Place praised the emperor for introducing the decimal system and genuinely understanding the emotional importance of common standardized measures and weights. Some may recognize Napoleon as the real inventor of our still rather modest and very continental euro. In the meantime, British scientists who regard the English Channel as a clear boundary vis-á-vis Europe claimed to have discovered old Roman streets on their island, which, in their view, proved that in good old Roman times the Roman emperors drove on the left side of the road.

But Napoleon's violent efforts ended in the Congress of Vienna, with nations uniting through a system of balance of power. The revolutions of 1848 once again evidenced conflicts between ideas and reality in Europe. Beginning with a sense of common European ideals they ended with a confirmation of national identities. Later, nationalism at its worst led in our century to the European civil wars widening into world wars, both decided by the intervention of the United States of America. Very quickly after the First World War there was a growing perception—and I want to name Coudenhove-Kalergi and Ortega y Gasset—that European unification would be the only way to avoid further totalitarian temptations. Both of them underlined that to succeed any such endeavor must avoid defining nations by common blood, common language, or natural borders. Following Ernest Renan's arguments, they made the case for a common past and a common future as the substance of identity for a nation and for *Europe*. In other words: Glory and repentance as to the past, inspiring common challenges for the future. But another quarter century elapsed, and with it the most terrible and violent chapter of European history, before Jean Monnet and others could start, step by step, to build up a real European community. Over forty years of a divided continent under the constraints of the Cold War finally led to the historical point when the real

Europeanization of Europe could start: the year of 1989 with its courageous, gentle, nonviolent revolutions. When the wall came down in Berlin on November 9, 1989, the governing mayor of our capital simply stated: "Today we are the happiest people in the world." I think it was a valid description of our feeling. And never before had I experienced an event taking place on German soil where so many people around the globe shared our joy.

Much less enthusiasm marked our neighbors' feelings when German political unification followed, for very understandable reasons. Would they be reliable partners? Would the Germans now return to their old national seesaw policy in the center of the continent? But no euphoric new German nationalism emerged. There was complete unanimity among all political camps in Germany that after unification we wanted to be even more Europe-orientated and integrated than before.

I do not want to elaborate on the many discrepancies and difficulties which so obviously are still unsolved in Europe. How can any European country be denied the prospect of membership in the European Union, if it is a free democracy and if it is willing and able to accept the so-called European *acquis communitaire*? Of course it is true that there are enormous differences in economic and social development among so many European societies. But could we really wish or afford to accept, in the long run, a Europe half rich and half poor? How far do we intend to go geographically? How do we achieve the institutional reforms inside the Union, which we so badly need in view of the growing number of members? How are we to cope with burden-sharing and agricultural reform? How to proceed, slowly but steadily, to more than a common currency, namely to a common foreign policy and to a common European defense?

At the present time there seems to be more national noise in the European air than a common spirit. But we should not be misled. To build a common Europe is a historical ambition without precedence. We are moving very slowly. Despite our common roots in ancient Greek culture, Roman law, and Christian religion, there are so many different languages and traditions, habits and identities that the aim can be no more than a European Federation of Nations, not a United States of Europe.

In a historical perspective, however, the last fifty years of a converging Europe are a very short period and one full of miracles. Undoubtedly, some more will have to be produced. But we will simply be forced to find the way for new ones. The future Europe will consist of open societies. European stability will prevail only if there is stability in all its parts. Otherwise, our democracies could not survive. This is what we have to learn from all the conflicts of our times, from Northern Ireland to Kosovo. At the present time we are learning the hard way. But we will learn. There will be a division of emphasis and labor among the members of the Union. As we Germans will have better to understand the Mediterranean preoccupation of France and others, our Western neighbors will have to realize the compelling importance of the new members coming from the Eastern half. These countries have been "abducted." But we belong together. Warsaw and Prague, Budapest and Riga are no less European than Salamanca or Cologne, Amsterdam or Bologna.

It is among the special tasks for the Germans to build a relationship of deep, constructive cooperation with Poland. This Eastern neighbor of ours had been divided for almost 150 years. It regained its own sovereignty at the end of the First World War only to become the first victim with the highest losses in the Second World War. At the end the Polish borders were shifted to the west, as were Germany's, and placed under Soviet control. Reconciliation between Poland and Germany was the hardest and the most important task for my generation. Now for the first time in centuries we have the chance of joining together as good neighbors for the common European future. There is a quickly growing economic exchange. The Polish border is at a distance of only eighty kilometers from Berlin. One of the border cities is Frankfurt/Oder—the birthplace of Heinrich von Kleist. It used to be a German city on both sides of the river. Now we have founded a new university, called Viadrina, in Frankfurt. More than one-third of the students are Polish. On the other side of the river, in Slubice, formerly a part of Frankfurt, there is a Collegium Polonicum where professors from both countries work with Polish and German students. This certainly is but a small example. Yet, I have to admit that it was a heartwarming and encouraging experience for me to experience as guest professor at this place a truly merging young generation of two peoples who had only very recently emerged from one hundred years of hatred and bloodshed.

In order to cope with our European aims and obligations, we, the Germans, have to accomplish unification in the lives and minds of our own people. We are still under way with that project. Without any doubt it will succeed. But it is taking more time than anticipated. There are fairly simple reasons for this. For the East Germans practically everything is changing. The laws and regulations, the education system, the market economy, the social structure, everything is new. Under Communist rule kindergartens, schools, vocational training, and higher education as well as employment stood under state order and plan. Now there is freedom, a very precious gift indeed. But after so many decades of dictatorship it is an exhausting daily exercise to learn how to make the best use of one's own initiatives and responsibilities.

As to the West Germans, who make up four-fifths of the whole German population, they were very happy about unification and went on with their accustomed way of life as usual. To unite means to share. But as a legal obligation this applies to the federal budget rather than to the conscious participation of the ordinary Western citizen. And there is a pressing need to make the time-consuming effort to understand one another's lives under such different circumstances as existed—to understand in particular and to accept that the vast majority of the East Germans had been leading a decent existence under the Communist dictatorship, with an admirable sense of neighborly solidarity. There did exist a very honorable private life in a deeply inhuman political system. This may be hardly conceivable for many Westerners, but it is the truth, which is to be realized and respected for the sake of real unification.

We are, of course, one people. At the same time we live with open borders. Of our population there are approximately 9 percent foreigners staying with us. They are not only *Gastarbeiter* who came with their families on our invitation, but a large number of migrants, refugees, and asylum seekers—much more than in any other continental country. This is a very difficult situation to cope with—socially, economically, and culturally. Here again we have to learn and we are learning. Under the conditions of global developments, a new Germany in a new Europe will have to prove that we are able to live together peacefully in a multicultural society where one can be different without fear.

In this sense the future will have to be a time of peace and freedom. This is within our reach only if democracies will stand together globally. There is good reason for hope. The mere existence of freedom in the Western democracies was the main reason for the breakdown of most Communist dictatorships in our century, without war, almost without any violence. Freedom for every human being is the best, the greatest idea of human kind. It is impossible to suppress it permanently. Our example of freedom is the peaceful power by which we want to transform the world. Our values and means are democracy and science. But they are not our highest goods. The paramount value is the dignity of the human being. In view of this dignity we have to observe our daily democracy and our science constantly and critically. Let us look at freedom of speech. It is a precious democratic good. I do not think anyone here would like to restrict it. In your democracy freedom of speech is well protected in a sublime way by the First Amendment.

Freedom of speech is to remain protected even if it is being used to proclaim things full of nonsense, of hatred, of downright inhuman thoughts. In every free democracy we encounter such misuse. But are they democrats, those who misuse such democratic rights? Or does not freedom of speech charge every true democrat with the inescapable responsibility to use it for the purpose of peace with democratic respect vis-à-vis any neighbor? Freedom of speech is granted to the irresponsible ones in trust to a responsible majority. If there is anywhere a danger of anarchy arising out of a growing misuse by the irresponsible ones, this cannot be prevented by legal means limiting the freedom of speech. This would put a democracy in contradiction with itself. It is not the state, but the democratic society, the community of true democrats, that has to protect this freedom.

Democracy is a framework, not simply of liberal rights, but of obligations and responsibilities. Freedom and responsibility are inseparable. Goethe once stated that it would be presumptuous simply to declare oneself free. Without responsibility this would mean at the same time to be ready for subordination. There are well-known lines by the German poet Theodor Storm:

> *Der eine fragt, was kommt danach, der andere: ist es recht?*
> *Und also unterscheidet sich der Freie von dem Knecht.*

One asks, what comes next; the other: what is right?
And thus the free man distinguishes himself from the slave.

True freedom of a people is a result of education by the society. This can succeed only if there is a deep understanding that freedom for all depends on a share of responsibility by all. In this respect Goethe has been a great teacher.

Science as well has to be linked to our highest value, to human dignity. This cannot be achieved by state prescription. It rests with the responsibility of science itself. Permit me to deal with this problem by a possibly surprising argument: Chicago is looked upon as a mecca of architecture. Under the influence, among others, of Mies van der Rohe, this architecture takes advantage of abstract forms. American cities usually present rectangular figures, a very abstract geometry. Now here in Chicago other geometric forms have been added: circles, circle segments, triangles, the oval, the rhombus. It looks like a fascinating discussion taking place within geometry. But as manifold as abstract geometry may be, it will always remain in contrast to living nature. In contemporary Chicago great and magnificent parks surround abstract architecture. In almost all flights of stones there are trees and beautifully kept flowers. Wherever you find a few square yards of soil, you meet with green and flourishing spots. This is not a simple decoration of architecture, but rather a justification in a deeper sense. Nature and architecture enhance each other. We perceive forms of human abstraction as a polarity or rather as complementary to forms of life. This provides architecture with its own new meaning. In such a surrounding we feel connected both with abstract thinking and with life as such. What we need is the two together. This city that, I believe, is not by mere chance at the top of educational reform in the United States, has thus produced a symbol of how to deal in a human way with the abstract thinking of science as one of the fundaments of our future.

This has never been easy. Think of some complaints at the time when the Enlightenment broadened our horizons and promoted modern science. To give just one example—Giaccomo Leopardi, who deplored in the eighteenth century that the spirit of ancient times had been expelled: "Human kind had replaced the illusions of happiness with the pain of truth and can no longer find the way back to the naive strong poetry of the old times, untouched by scientific poison." Nobody would express such opinions today. Science has liberated us from dominating ideologies. This is an enormous progress. Science has conquered and changed the world. Yet not to ideologize science does not mean to accept science as the only origin of truth. There are other ways to come close to truth: philosophy, religion, human conscience, love, art. Science can serve us only as long as it is aware of its limitation in realizing truth.

Here again Goethe has been leading us into a new age. Throughout his life he warned against declaring science to be the only guardian of truth. His words were: "Denn das Leben ist die Liebe und des Lebens Leben Geist" (Life is love and the life of living is spirit). Time and again he urged that we never rely on freedom as a gift of nature sufficiently understood by us. With all the daily progress of science and technology we have to cope anew with conditions of freedom. Democracy and science are at their best as long as they remain aware of all the dangers immanent within themselves in order to redefine and restore freedom permanently.

"Nur der verdient sich Freiheit wie das Leben, der täglich sie erobern muß" (The only ones who deserve freedom are those who struggle daily for it). In 1949 Albert Schweitzer addressed the Goethe bicentennial conference and opened the Aspen Institute in Colorado.

His message was the awe of life, of all life—the very awe that took him to the African jungle to save the lives of human beings there. Democracy is built upon awe of human life. It is the essence of Goethe's poetic work to let every human being experience awe vis-à-vis himself and any other person:

> *Und wenn mich am Tag die Ferne lauer Berge sehnlich zieht,*
> *Nachts das Übermaß der Sterne prächtig mir zu Häupten glüht,*
> *Alle Tag und alle Nächte preis ich so des Menschen Los:*
> *Setzt er ewig sich ins Rechte, ist er ewig schön und groß.*

> And if, during the day, the distant mountains draw me ardently,
> At night the expanse of stars glows majestically overhead;
> Day and night I praise the lot of human beings—
> When they are eternally just, they are eternally beautiful and
>   grand.

WHAT IS THE FUTURE OF GERMAN IMMIGRATION POLICY?

GERMAN IMMIGRATION POLICY—PAST, PRESENT, AND FUTURE

Barbara John

When Richard von Weizsäcker became mayor of Berlin in 1981, he installed the office of the Commissioner for Foreigners' Affairs—the very first of its kind at the state level—and the government appointed me to run this new administration. I can well remember at the time answering snide questions as to the prospective length of my service. I tried to give a well-founded and honest answer, claiming that by the end of the 1980s my special mission should be completed.

My prediction was based not only on the numbers of immigrants arriving and leaving; it was also based on the general assumption derived from the officially declared federal policy that Germany is not a country of immigration and does not intend to become one. Thus the ongoing inflow of family members of immigrants at the beginning of the 1980s seemed to be the end of the large immigration flows that had started in 1955, when Germany agreed to temporary labor immigration from Italy. Six years later a second agreement was signed with Turkey, followed by agreements with other Mediterranean countries, such as Spain, Tunisia, and Greece. Immigration did not end in the 1950s, of course; nor was what I once referred to as my "special mission" completed by the end of the 1980s. Let us now take a look at what happened instead of an end to immigration into Germany.

There was a sharp increase in the numbers of immigrants until 1973, when a ban was placed on further labor immigration due to rising unemployment in Germany. The rise in immigration at the beginning of the eighties was due to programs for family unification. A voluntary return program designed for Turkish immigrants and their families caused a decline in immigration numbers beginning in 1983. Under the federal program, unemployed immigrants could receive a lump sum of capitalized unemployment benefits.

Since 1989, when all borders between Central and Eastern European countries opened up, a steady flow of asylum seekers and refugees, including 350,000 war refugees from Bosnia-Herzegovina, began to enter into Germany. At present, about 110,000 refugees from Kosovo are living in Germany under a temporary protection regime.

One can easily call it a political irony that a self-professed country of nonimmigration now has a greater percentage of foreign-born persons (13 percent—including ethnic Germans) than the United States (9 percent), a self-professed "nation of immigrants." Following the United States, Germany now has the second greatest numbers of immigrants of any country in the world. Given the fact that once immigration starts it is self-perpetuating due to networking effects among immigrant groups, immigrants will continue to enter Germany in significant numbers in the coming years. Germany receives about 300,000 persons per year, fully one-half of the total number of 600,000 who arrive in all of the member states of the EU combined.

Seventy percent of all Turkish emigrants living in Western Europe now live in Germany, a total of 2.2 million immigrants. Since 170,000 Turks are living in Berlin, the German capital is also the largest Turkish city in the world outside of Turkey. Never before in the history of the German nation has the population been more diverse—culturally, religiously, and linguistically. But the notion of Germany as a multicultural society is hardly accepted yet in Germany. To be more precise: except for the migrant groups and the activists in the field, this notion is still rejected, often fiercely. Let me illustrate this: exactly one year ago, in

June 1998, a public debate stirred up the city of Berlin and the entire country. The theme of the debate can be summarized thus: in Germany the cultural mainstream has to be fabricated out of German values (*deutsche Leitkultur*) in order to overcome the detrimental influences that go along with a multicultural society.

The former Berlin senator of the interior, who contended that integration policies simply did not work, triggered the discussion. In support of this claim, he noted that: (1) unemployment among the ethnic minorities is nearly three times higher than among the German population; (2) the concentration of immigrant families in some local communities is far too high; (3) many immigrants don't acquire proper proficiency in the German language; and (4) the Muslim faith, shared by large immigrant groups, is alien to the majority culture.

"You don't find Germany any more in the local community of Kreuzberg," the senator declared in an interview published in *Bild-Zeitung*, the leading tabloid paper in Germany. In order better to understand the underlying meaning of his remark, one should be aware that in Kreuzberg, an inner-city area in Berlin, 34 percent of the population come from immigrant groups. The senator contended that we should not consider these issues taboo, but rather admit that the idea of a multicultural Germany denies, even denigrates, the German culture. Leftist intellectuals who seek to destroy the German identity could see multiculturalism as a last-ditch effort.

I mention this event because it serves as an eye-opener, enabling a better understanding of the German dilemma concerning the issues of immigration, integration, and becoming a multicultural society. It might not come as a surprise that the vast majority of the German population wholeheartedly agreed with the minister. The idea of a *Leitkultur* is widely supported and quite popular. It is not, however, universally shared. A debate sparked by the senator's remarks ensued in the weekly newspaper *Die Zeit* and in many local dailies about the political and social implications of these arguments. More pointedly, the discussion revolved around the challenges that lie ahead in creating and managing a German nation-state in which the existence of many cultures is widely accepted and is no longer seen in juxtaposition to a German culture or even as a threat to it. What, then, needs to be done?

First: a new outlook toward immigration and immigrants. If a country like Germany, which already has in place a rigid program to avoid permanent immigration, turns out to be the largest immigrant nation in the European Union, something must be done to indicate that the government is in control of the situation. To put it quite pointedly: either you change your mentality or you change your immigration flow drastically.

Since the latter proposal raises unsolvable problems for the time being in Germany, the political elites should rather adopt a brighter view of what is happening. Additionally, there should be better immigration management. There are many reasons why this strategy could easily be adopted. Only a terribly narrow view could deny that some immigrant groups are still facing difficulties in education and in the economy. But, if you look closely at the situation, you discover, alongside the ways in which the immigrants themselves bear responsibility, many homemade, systemic causes for some of the failures.

Immigrant spouses, for example, who join their non-German partners, are not entitled to a work permit for a period of four years after their arrival in Germany. The first stamp they get in their visas reads: "No permission to work." How are they supposed to learn the language, mix with other people, and get better vocational training? Due to our paternalistic views, the welfare-benefit registration list is open to them, but not the labor market.

Why not look at those who made it because there were fewer barriers? Take, for instance, the tens of thousands of what I call the "Tuypies"—Turkish urban young professionals. They are self-made businesspeople, successful students, engineers, and media people. There would be many more of them if we were ready to abolish some of the outdated regulations that still inhibit the opening of new businesses.

Outdated legal provisions are not unique to the labor market. A scholar at the University of Chicago, Isabell Stein-Pyritz, once told me about her ongoing struggle with the German naming-laws. She wanted to give her daughter—a dual citizen of Germany and the United States—the middle name "Stein," in order to preserve her family name. Her case is now pending at the German constitutional court in Karlsruhe!

With the new citizenship law coming into effect in January 2000 we have the opportunity to finally overcome the German obsession with homogeneity. For the first time in our history, children born in Germany whose parents are foreign nationals will automatically get German citizenship. At the age of eighteen, however, they have to decide whether they want to keep their German nationality. Should they choose to preserve their German citizenship, the citizenship they received from their parent(s) must be renounced.

I am quite sure that the new *jus soli* will work as an active leveler in our society—legally and socially. No longer will there be an arbitrary division in schools along passport lines. No longer will young Turks be able to opt out of military service or the social service equivalent. No longer will children born in Germany be issued limited resident permits. With the *jus soli*, the human differences of culture, language, religion, and ethnicity will become an everyday fact of public life.

The fact of diversity and multiculturalism can no longer be denied or deferred when one ponders German identity. With millions of immigrants already, Germany has now joined those societies that are seen as attractive nations to live in. This is not only a much better option than to be a nation of emigrants (many Germans still remember the terrifying implications of forced emigration), it will also promote the development of German democracy more fully in the direction of a more pluralistic and more republican civil society.

Let me end this discussion with a quote from Goethe, who must have foreseen this occasion. "Der Deutsche," he wrote in his *Maxims and Reflections*, "soll alle Sprachen lernen, damit ihm zu Hause kein Fremder unbequem, er aber in der Fremde überall zu Hause ist." Today the term culture is perhaps more applicable to what Goethe meant to say. In English his recommendation might therefore read: "Germans should learn to understand other cultures so that at home no foreigner is felt to be a burden and they [the Germans] can feel at home everywhere in the world."

BEYOND SOVEREIGNTY:
DE FACTO TRANSNATIONALISM IN
IMMIGRATION POLICY[1]

Saskia Sassen

While the state continues to play the most important role in immigration policy making and implementation, the state itself has been transformed by the growth of a global economic system and other transnational processes. These have brought on conditions that bear on the state's regulatory role and its autonomy. Two particular aspects of this development are of significance to the role of the state in immigration policy making and implementation: One is the relocation of various components of state authority to supranational organizations such as the institutions of the European Union, the newly formed World Trade Organization, or the international human rights code. A second is the de facto privatization of various governance functions as a result of the privatization of public sector activities and of economic deregulation. This privatization assumes particular meanings in the context of the internationalization of trade and investment. Corporations, markets, and free trade agreements are now in charge of "governing" an increasing share of cross-border flows, including cross-border flows of specialized professional workers as part of international trade and investment in services.

The major implication for immigration policy is that these developments have had an impact on the sovereignty of the state and, further, that the state itself has been a participant in the implementation of many of these new arrangements. The state has contributed to the formation of the global economic system and has furthered the consensus around the pursuit of economic globalization. Both the impact on the state's sovereignty and the state's participation in the new global economic system have transformed the state itself, affected the power of different agencies within it, and furthered the internationalization of the inter-state system through a proliferation of bi- and multilateral agreements.

Immigration policy is deeply embedded in the question of state sovereignty and the inter-state system. As a result it is no longer sufficient simply to assert the sovereign role of the state in immigration policy design and implementation; it is necessary to examine also the transformation of the state itself and what that can entail for migration policy and the regulation of migration flows and settlement. As I argue in the book from which this paper is drawn, it is becoming important to factor in the possibility of declining state sovereignty precisely because the state is a major actor in immigration policy and regulation. Nor is it sufficient simply to assert that globalization has brought with it a declining significance of the state in economic regulation. Why? Because the state has been a participant in this process and is the strategic institution for the legislative changes and innovations necessary for economic globalization as we know it today.

This may seem far removed from the question of immigration policy. But we need to expand the analytic terrain within which we examine the options in immigration policy making in the highly developed countries. And we cannot simply use the state as a background fact, a given.

One of the crucial issues in the transformation of the state that is relevant to immigration policy making has to do with the enormous work of legal innovation necessary for the formation of a global economy. The global economy is both a set of practices and a set of legal innovations within which to encase those practices. Economic globalization has created a new geography of power within which the state finds its sovereign power reconstituted, often diminished. And it has contributed to the formation of new legal regimes and much legal and policy innovation, much of it representing a relocation of authority away from the state.

Immigration policy making, in contrast, has suffered from a lack of innovation in most highly developed countries, with the exception of the work around the formation of the European Union and free trade agreements such as NAFTA and the Uruguay Round of the GATT. In the case of Europe, such policy changes as free movement within the Union and the shift of some immigration policy components to the European level, have required considerable innovation in international law. NAFTA and WTO required the formation of specialized regimes for the circulation of service and other kinds of providers; this is likely to include individuals, particularly in the case of many services. These regimes within NAFTA and WTO can be seen as containing a form of "migrant worker policy," one that is addressed to highly specialized workers and is a privatized regime.

These are the issues briefly discussed in the paper. One argument that organizes the paper is that this reconfiguration has brought with it a de facto transnationalism in the handling of a growing number of immigration issues, both domestically and internationally. This can take many forms: the shift of certain elements of immigration policy onto supranational institutions in the European Union; the sharp increase in the extent and content of collaboration in the U.S.-Mexico Binational Immigration Commission; the rapid increase in the use of international human rights instruments by judges adjudicating on immigration and refugee questions in both Europe and the United States; and the already mentioned formation of a privatized regime for the circulation of service workers in the major free-trade agreements as part of the liberalization of international trade and investment in services. I consider these and other developments a de facto trans- nationalism because they are fragmented, incipient, and have not been fully captured at the most formal levels of international public law and conventions, nor in national representations of the sovereign state. My argument is, then, that there is more on-the-ground transnationalism than hits the formal eye.

In order to develop this particular way of framing the evidence it is important first to bring some precision to concepts such as economic globalization and transnationalism and their impact on the sovereignty and exclusive territoriality of national states. This is the subject of a first, very brief section, confined largely to states operating under the rule of law. The second and third sections focus on the constraints faced by the state in highly developed countries in the making of immigration policy today.

The State and the New Economic Regime

Two notions underlie much of the discussion about globalization. One is the proposition that what the global economy gains, the national state loses and vice versa. The other is the proposition that if an event (from a business transaction to a judicial decision) takes place in a national territory it is a national event. In other words, dualism and geography (in a narrow territorial sense) are the hallmarks of this type of under-standing.

But there is by now a considerable body of scholarship that has shown us that the spatiality of the global economy does not simply lie somewhere in the interstices between states. To a good extent global processes and institutional arrangements materialize in national terri-tories; even the most digitized global financial market is grounded in a set of very material resources and spaces largely embedded in national territories. As has been said often, one of the key properties of the cur-rent phase in the long history of the world economy is the ascendance of information technologies, the associated increase in the mobility and liquidity of capital, and the resulting decline in the regulatory capaci-ties of national states over key sectors of their economies. This is well illustrated by the case of the leading information, financial, and advanced corporate service industries. These tend to have a space econ-omy that is transnational and is partly embedded in electronic spaces that override conventional jurisdictions and boundaries.

Yet, this is also a space economy which reveals the need for strategic sites with vast concentrations of resources and infrastructure, sites that are situated in national territories and are far less mobile than much of the general commentary on the global economy suggests. The excessive emphasis on the hypermobility and liquidity of capital is a partial account. We need to distinguish between the capacity for global transmission/communication and the material conditions that make this possible, between the globalization of the financial industry and the array of resources—from buildings to labor inputs—that makes this possible; and so on for other sectors as well.[2] Place is central to the multiple circuits through which economic globalization is constituted. One strategic type of place for these developments is the global city.[3]

As a consequence of this embedding of global processes in national territories, notably in global cities, one of the key features of the role of the state vis-à-vis economic globalization (unlike earlier forms of the global economy) has been to negotiate the intersection of national law and foreign actors—whether firms, markets, or individuals. We generally use the term "deregulation" to describe the outcome of this negotiation. The problem with this term is that it only captures the withdrawal of the state from regulating its economy. It does not register all the ways in which the state participates in setting up the new frameworks through which globalization is furthered; nor does it capture the associated transformations inside the state.

Coding everything that involves the national state, as an instance of the national, is simply inadequate. The theoretical and methodological challenge presented by the current phase of globalization is that it entails a transcending of exclusive national territoriality and of the interstate system yet is implanted in national territories and institutions. Hence globalization directly engages two marking features of the nation-state: exclusive territoriality and sovereignty.

Similarly, the emergent international human rights regime engages territoriality and sovereignty. What matters here is not so much the moral force of the idea, but the far more practical fact of a rapid multiplication of instruments available to judges and the build-up of case law where this applies, as in the United States for example. The key issue here is the fact that international regimes or codes, such as human rights, largely become operative in national courts. One could of course simply assert that in such cases we are dealing with what is ultimately a national institution. To do so means discounting even the possibility that the ascendance of such international regimes engages the sovereignty and territoriality of the national state. And since the multiplication of instruments and their growing use by national courts is a very recent development—unlike the concept of human rights—we must at least allow for the possibility that there are new processes afoot also in this realm.

In terms of sovereignty, the emergent consensus in the community of states to further globalization has created a set of specific obligations on participating states. The state remains as the ultimate guarantor of the "rights" of global capital, i.e., the protection of contracts and property rights. Thus the state has incorporated the global project of its own shrinking role in regulating economic transactions. Firms operating transnationally want to ensure the functions traditionally exercised by the state in the national realm of the economy, notably guaranteeing property rights and contracts. The state here can be conceived of as representing a technical administrative capacity, which cannot be replicated at this time by any other institutional arrangement; furthermore, this is a capacity backed by military power, with global power in the case of some states.

Deregulation and other policies furthering economic globalization cannot simply be considered as an instance of a declining significance of the state. Deregulation is a vehicle through which a growing number of states are furthering economic globalization and guaranteeing the rights of global capital, an essential ingredient of the former. Deregulation and kindred policies constitute the elements of a new legal regime dependent on consensus among states to further globalization. This manner of conceptualizing deregulation suggests that the duality national-global as mutually exclusive is problematic in that it does not adequately represent what economic globalization has actually entailed for national states.

While central, the role of the state in producing the legal encasements for economic globalization is no longer as exclusive as it was in earlier periods. Economic globalization has also been accompanied by the creation of new legal regimes and legal practices and the expansion and renovation of some older forms that bypass national legal systems. Among the most important ones in the private sector today are international commercial arbitration and the variety of institutions that fulfill rating and advisory functions that have become essential for the operation of the global economy.

These and other such transnational institutions and regimes do raise questions about the relation between state sovereignty and the governance of global economic processes. International commercial arbitration is basically a private justice system and credit-rating agencies are private gate-keeping systems. Along with other such institutions they have emerged as important governance mechanisms whose authority is not centered in the state. They contribute to maintain order at the top, one could say.

All of this had an impact on sovereignty and on the mutually exclusive territoriality that has marked the history of the modern state. This is an extremely complex and highly differentiated history that cannot be adequately described here. There is an enormously rich scholarship on this subject.[4]

There are two points I would want to emphasize about this history here because they are relevant to the subject of this paper, particularly the notion that we may need considerable innovation in immigration policy given today's major transformations. One of these points is the fact that at various periods of major transitions there was a coexistence of multiple systems of rule. This was the case, for instance in the transition from the medieval system of rule to the modern state.[5] And it may well be the case today in this period of transition to a global economy. As I will argue later, supranational organizations today and regimes such as GATT and NAFTA may well signal the strengthening of other nonexclusive systems of rule today. A second element in the history of the modern state that matters here is the fact of enormous contestation to the formation of and claims by central states. Again I see this as relevant to the contemporary period in that it signals the possibility of regimes that go beyond state sovereignty or that involve far more developed instances of multilateralism notwithstanding strong resistance among policy makers and analysts to even the idea of such a possibility.

While these new conditions for transnational economies are being produced and implemented by governments and economic actors in highly developed countries, immigration policy in those same countries remains centered in older conceptions about control and regulation. One of the key obstacles to even beginning to think along totally different lines about immigration policy is the widespread conviction that any approach other than border control would lead to massive invasions from the Third World. Much general commentary and policy making tends to proceed, wittingly or not, as if most people in less developed countries want to go to a rich country, as if all immigrants want to become permanent settlers, as if the problem of current immigration policy has to do basically with gaps or failures in enforcement, as if raising the levels of border control is an effective way of regulating immigration. This type of understanding of immigration clearly leads to a certain type of immigration policy, one centered on the fear of being invaded by people from less developed countries everywhere and hence on border control as the only answer. The evidence on immigration shows that most people do not want to leave their countries, that overall levels of permanent immigration are not very large, that there is considerable circulation and return migration, that most migration flows eventually stabilize if not decline. Making these the central facts about the reality of immigration should allow for a broader set of options when it comes to immigration policy than would be the case with mass emigration and invasion.

But can the state escape its own transformation and the pressures towards transnationalism when it comes to immigration policy design and implementation?

Beyond Sovereignty: Constraints on States' Policy Making

When it comes to immigration policy, states under the rule of law increasingly confront a range of rights and obligations, pressures from both inside and outside, from universal human rights to not so universal ethnic lobbies.

First, we see emerging a de facto regime, centered in international agreements and conventions as well as in various rights gained by immigrants, that limits the state's role in controlling immigration. An example of such an agreement is the International Convention adopted by the General Assembly of the UN on December 18, 1990, on the protection of the rights of all migrant workers and members of their families (Resolution 45/158).

Further, there is a set of rights of resident immigrants widely upheld by legal authorities. We have also seen the gradual expansion over the last three decades of civil and social rights to marginal populations, whether women, ethnic minorities, or immigrants and refugees.

In this context, the new 1996 U.S. immigration law, which curtails the rights of undocumented and legal immigrants, can be seen as a rejection of these international instruments. Nonetheless, precisely because these instruments exist the stage is set for at least some contestation. We have seen this frequently in the long and arduous history of international human rights codes. The extension of rights, which has taken place mostly through the judiciary, has confronted states with a number of constraints in the area of immigration and refugee policy. For instance, there have been legislative attempts in France and Germany to limit family reunification, attempts which were blocked by administrative and constitutional courts on the grounds that such restrictions would violate international agreements. The courts have also regularly supported a combination of rights of resident immigrants, which have the effect of limiting the government's power over resident immigrants. Similarly such courts have limited the ability of governments to restrict or stop asylum seekers from entering the country.

Efforts that mix the conventions on universal human rights and national judiciaries assume many different forms. Some of the instances in the United States are the sanctuary movement in the 1980s which sought to establish protected areas, typically in churches, for refugees from Central America; judicial battles, such as those around the status of Salvadorans granted indefinite stays though formally defined as illegal; and the fight for the rights of detained Haitians in an earlier wave of boat lifts. It is clear that notwithstanding the lack of an enforcement apparatus, human rights limit the discretion of states in how they treat nonnationals on their territory. It is also worth noting in this regard that UNHCR is the only UN agency with a universally conceded right of access to a country experiencing a refugee crisis.

The growing influence of international human rights law is particularly evident in Europe. It was not until the 1980s that a similar influence began in the United States, where it still lags behind.[6] This has been seen partly as a result of American definitions of personhood that have led courts in some cases to address the matter of undocumented immigrants within American constitutionalism, notably the idea of inalienable and natural rights of people and persons, without territorial confines. The emphasis on persons makes possible interpretations about undocumented immigrants in a way it would not if the emphasis were on citizens. It was not until the mid-1970s and the early 1980s that domestic courts began to consider human rights codes as normative instruments in their own right. The rapid growth of undocumented immigration and the sense of the state's incapacity to control the flow and to regulate the various categories in its population was a factor leading courts to consider the international human rights regime; it allows courts to rule on basic protections of individuals not formally accounted in the national territory and legal system, notably undocumented aliens and unauthorized refugees.[7]

The growing accountability, in principle, of states under the rule of law to international human rights codes and institutions, together with the fact that individuals and nonstate actors can make claims on those states in terms of those codes, signals a development that goes beyond the expansion of human rights within the framework of nation-states.

It contributes to redefining the bases of legitimacy of states under the rule of law and the notion of nationality. Under human rights regimes states must increasingly take account of persons qua persons, rather than qua citizens. The individual is now an object of law and a site for rights regardless of whether a citizen or an alien.[8]

Finally, the numbers and kinds of political actors involved in immigration policy debates and policy making in Western Europe, North America, and Japan are far greater than they were two decades ago: the European Union, anti-immigrant parties, vast networks of organizations in both Europe and North America that often represent immigrants, or claim to do so, and fight for immigrant rights, immigrant associations and immigrant politicians, mostly in the second generation, and, especially in the United States, so-called ethnic lobbies.[9] The policy process for immigration is no longer confined to a narrow governmental arena of ministerial and administrative interaction. Public opinion and public political debate have become part of the arena wherein immigration policy is shaped.[10] Whole parties position themselves politically in terms of their stand on immigration, especially in some of the European countries.

These developments are particularly evident in the case of the European Union.[11] Europe's single market program has had a powerful impact in raising the prominence of various issues associated with free circulation of people as an essential element in creating a frontier-free community; earlier EC institutions lacked the legal competence to deal with many of these issues but had to begin to address them. Gradually EC institutions wound up more deeply involved with visa policy, family reunification, and migration policy—all formerly exclusively in the domain of the individual national states. National governments resisted EC (and later EU) involvement in these once exclusively national domains. But now both legal and practical issues have made such involvement acceptable and inevitable notwithstanding many public pronouncements to the contrary.

It is becoming evident that many aspects of immigration and refugee policy intersect with EU legal competence. A key nexus here is the free movement of persons and attendant social rights as part of the formation of a single market. In practice the EU is assuming an increasingly important role, and the fact that immigration is a long-term feature in these countries is slowly being acknowledged. The monetary and economic union would require greater flexibility in movement of workers and their families and thereby pose increasing problems for national immigration laws regarding non-EU nationals in EU member states. There is now growing recognition for the need of an EU-wide immigration policy, something denied for a long time by individual states.

In the case of the United States, the combination of forces at the governmental level is quite different yet has similar general implications about the state's constraints in immigration policy making. Immigration policy in the United States is today largely debated and shaped by Congress, and hence is highly public and subject to a vast multiplicity of local interests, notably ethnic lobbies.[12] This has made it a very public process, quite different from other processes of policy making.[13]

The fact that immigration in the United States has historically been the preserve of the federal government assumes new meaning in today's context of radical devolution—the return of powers to the states.[14] Although political and constitutional arguments for reallocating federal power to the states are not new, the recent reemergence of the Tenth Amendment as a politically viable and popular guideline is a major political shift since the New Deal in the relations between the federal government and the states. There is now an emerging conflict between several state governments and the federal government around the particular issue of federal mandates concerning immigrants—such as access to public health care and schools—without mandatory federal funding. Thus states with disproportionate shares of immigrants are asserting that they are disproportionately burdened by the putative costs of immigration. In the United States the costs of immigration are an area of great debate and wide-ranging estimates.[15] At the heart of this conflict is the fact that the federal government sets policy but does not assume responsibility, financial or otherwise, for the implementation of many key aspects of immigration policy. The radical devolution under way now is going to accentuate some of these divisions further.

States are beginning to request reimbursement from the federal government for the costs of benefits and services that they are required to provide, especially to undocumented immigrants. In 1994, six states (Arizona, California, Florida, New Jersey, New York, and Texas) filed separate suits in federal district courts to recover costs they claim to have sustained because of the federal government's failure to enforce U.S. immigration policy, protect the nation's borders, and provide adequate resources for immigration emergencies.[16] The amounts range from $50.5 million in New Jersey for FY 1993 costs of imprisoning five hundred undocumented criminal felons and future costs for construction of new detention facilities, to $33.6 billion in New York for all state and county costs associated with undocumented immigration between 1988 to 1993. U.S. District Court judges have dismissed all six lawsuits; some of the states are appealing the decisions. The conflict is illustrated by the notorious case of the state of California and its $377 million lawsuit against the federal government. The radical devolution under way now is going to accentuate some of these divisions further.

One of the questions raised by these developments concerns the nature of the control by national states in regulating immigration. The question here is not so much one of how effective is a state's control over its borders—we know it is never absolute. The question concerns rather the substantive nature of state control over immigration given international human rights agreements, the extension of various social and political rights to resident immigrants over the last twenty years, and the multiplication of political actors involved with the immigration question.

We can illuminate the issue of the substantive nature of the control by states over immigration with a twist on the zero sum argument. If a government closes one kind of entry category, recent history shows that another one will have a rise in numbers. A variant on this dynamic is that if a government has, for instance, a very liberal policy on asylum, public opinion may turn against all asylum seekers and close up the country totally; this in turn is likely to promote an increase in irregular entries.[17]

When Different Regimes Intersect

Immigration policy continues to be characterized by its formal isolation from other major processes, as if it were possible to handle migration as a bounded, closed event.

There are, one could say, two major epistemic communities—one concerning the flow of capital and information; the other, immigration. Both of these epistemic communities are international, and both enjoy widespread consensus in the community of states.

The coexistence of such different regimes for capital and for immigrants has not been seen as an issue in the United States. The case of the EU is of interest here because it represents an advanced stage of formalization, and in this effort European states are discovering the difficulties if not impossibility of maintaining two such diverse regimes. The European Community and the national governments of member states have found the juxtaposition of the divergent regimes for immigration flows and for other types of flows rather difficult to handle. The discussion, design, and implementation of policy aimed at forming a European Union make it evident that immigration policy has to account for the facts of rapid economic internationalization. The European Union shows us with great clarity the moment when states need to confront this contradiction in their design of formal policy frameworks. The other major regional systems in the world are far from that moment and may never reach it. Yet they contain less formalized versions of the juxtaposition between border-free economies and border controls to keep immigrants out. NAFTA is one such instance, as are, in a more diffuse way, various initiatives for greater economic integration in the Western Hemisphere.

Though less clearly than in Western Europe, these issues are present in other regions with cross-border migrations. These are regional systems constituted partly as zones of influence of major economic or geopolitical powers, e.g., the long-term dominance of the United States over the Caribbean Basin. What matters here is that to a good extent major international migration flows have been embedded in one or another variant of these regional systems. The quasi-transnational economic integration characterizing such regional systems produces its own variety of contradictions between drives for border-free economic spaces and for border control to keep immigrants and refugees out.

There are strategic sites where it becomes clear that the existence of two very different regimes for the circulation of capital and the circulation of immigrants poses problems that cannot be solved through the old rules of the game, where the facts of transnationalization weigh in on the state's decisions regarding immigration. For instance the need to create special regimes for the circulation of service workers both within GATT and NAFTA as part of the further internationalization of trade and investment in services. This regime for the circulation of service workers has been uncoupled from any notion of migration; but it represents in fact a version of temporary labor migration. It is a regime for labor mobility that is in good part under the oversight of entities that are quite autonomous from the government. This points to an institutional reshuffling of some of the components of sovereign power over entry and can be seen as an extension of the general set of processes whereby state sovereignty is partly being decentered onto other non- or quasi-governmental entities for the governance of the global economy.[18]

The development of provisions for workers and businesspersons signals the difficulty of *not* dealing with the circulation of people in the implementation of free trade and investment frameworks. In their own specific ways each of these efforts—NAFTA, GATT, and the European Union—has had to address cross-border labor circulation.

One instantiation of the impact of globalization on governmental policy making can be seen in Japan's new immigration law passed in 1990. While this is quite different from how the issue plays in the context of free trade agreements, it nonetheless illustrates one way of handling the need for cross-border circulation of professional workers in a context of resistance to the notion of open borders. This legislation opened the country to several categories of highly specialized professionals with a Western background (e.g., experts in international finance, Western-style accounting, Western medicine, etc.) in recognition of the growing internationalization of the professional world in Japan; it made the entry of what is referred to as "simple labor" illegal. This can be read as importing "Western human capital" and closing borders to immigrants.

Further, the need to address cross-border circulation of people has also become evident in free trade agreements in the less-developed world, notably in Latin America. There has been a sharp increase in activity around the international circulation of people in each of the major regional trading blocks: Mercosur, the Grupo Andino, and the Mercado Comun de Centroamerica. In the early 1990s each one launched a variety of initiatives concerning international labor migration among their member countries. This was in many ways a new development. Some of the founding treaties preceded the flurry of meetings on labor migrations and the circulation of people. But it is clear that conditions in the early 1990s forced this issue on the agenda. When one examines what actually happened it becomes evident that the common markets for investment and commerce in each of these regions had themselves become activated under the impact of globalization, deregulation, privatization. It was the increased circulation of capital, goods, and information under the impact of globalization, deregulation, and privatization that forced the question of the circulation of people on the agenda.

In the case of the United States and its major immigration source country, Mexico, it appears that the signing of NAFTA has also had the effect of activating a series of new initiatives regarding migration—a sort of de facto bilateralism that represents a radically new phase in the handling of migration between these two countries. It is worth providing some detail on these.

Not unlike what was the case in Latin America, we are seeing a reactivation of older instruments and a flurry of new activity around the question of international migration. To provide better coordination between the two countries Presidents Carter and Lopez Portillo established the U.S.-Mexico Consultative Mechanism. This eventually led to the formation of the U.S.-Mexico Binational Commission in 1981 to serve as a forum for meetings between Cabinet-level officials from both countries. It was conceived as a flexible mechanism that would meet once or twice a year. One of the earliest working groups formed was the Border Relations Action group, again in 1981.

What is different over the last two years is the frequency, focus, and actual work that is getting done in the meetings of the working groups. NAFTA has further contributed to strengthening the contacts and collaboration in the working groups. Particularly active is the working group on Migration and Consular Affairs.[19] There are also disagreements between the two delegations, which are discussed openly. Notably, the Mexican delegation is deeply concerned about the growing anti-immigrant feeling and measures in the United States. The U.S. delegation has agreed to work together to combat these developments. The Mexican delegation also expressed concern at the U.S. proposal to expand and strengthen border fences to improve security in various locations. They emphasized the negative effects of such a measure on the border communities and Mexican efforts to resolve the problems in the most troubled locations. Notwithstanding these serious disagreements, and perhaps precisely because of them, both delegations are convinced of the necessity to continue the collaboration and communication that has developed over the last two years.

All of these developments have the effect of (a) reducing the autonomy of the state in immigration policy making and (b) multiplying the sectors within the state that are addressing immigration policy and therewith multiplying the room for conflicts within the state. The assertion that the state is in charge of immigration policy is less and less helpful. Policy making regarding international issues can engage very different parts of the government. The state itself has not only been transformed by its participation in the global economy, but has of course never been a homogeneous actor. It is constituted through multiple agencies and social forces. Indeed it could be said that although the state has central control over immigration policy, the work of exercising that claimed power often begins with a limited contest between the state and interested social forces. These interest groups include agribusiness, manufacturing, humanitarian groups, unions, ethnic organizations, and zero population growth efforts. Today we need to add to this the fact that the furthering of economic globalization is reconfiguring the hierarchies of power and influence within the state.[20]

The conditions within which immigration policy is being made and implemented today range from the pressures of economic globalization and its implications for the role of the state to international agreements on human rights. And the institutional settings within which immigration policy is being made and implemented ranges from national states and local states to supranational organizations.

Why does this transformation of the state and the inter-state system matter for the regulation of immigration? The displacement of governance functions away from the state to nonstate entities affects the state's capacity to control or keep controlling its borders. New systems of governance are being created. Increasingly they may create conflicts with the state's capacity to keep on regulating immigration in traditional ways. Further, the transformation of the state itself through its role in the implementation of global processes may well contribute to new constraints, options, and vested interests. The ascendance of agencies linked to furthering globalization and the decline of those linked to domestic equity questions is quite likely to eventually have an effect on the immigration agenda.

Conclusion

The developments described here point to a number of trends that may become increasingly important for sound immigration policy making. First, where the effort toward the formation of transnational economic spaces has gone the furthest and been most formalized it has become very clear that existing frameworks for immigration policy are problematic. It is not the case that the coexistence of very different regimes for the circulation of capital and for that of people is free of tension and contention. This is most evident in the legislative work necessary for the formation of the European Union. Lesser versions of this tension are evident in the need to design special provisions for the circulation of workers in all the major free trade agreements.

Second, we see the beginning of a displacement of government functions onto nongovernmental or quasi-governmental institutions. This is most evident in the new transnational legal and regulatory regimes created in the context of economic globalization. But it is also intersecting with questions of migration, specifically temporary labor migration, as is evident in the creation of special regimes for the circulation of service workers and businesspersons within both GATT and NAFTA as part of the further internationalization of trade and investment in services. This regime for the circulation of service workers has been separated from any notion of migration, but it represents in fact a version of temporary labor migration. It is a regime for labor mobility that is in good part under the oversight of entities that are quite autonomous from the government. We can see in this displacement the elements of a privatization of certain aspects of the regulation of cross-border labor mobility. Third, the legitimization process for states under the rule of law calls for respect and enforcement of international human rights codes, regardless of the nationality and legal status of an individual. While enforcement is precarious, it nonetheless signals a major shift in the legitimization process. This is perhaps most evident in the strategic role that the judiciary has assumed in the highly developed countries when it comes to the rights of immigrants, refugees, and asylum seekers.

Finally, the state itself has been transformed by this combination of developments. This is so partly because the state under the rule of law is one of the key institutional arenas for the implementation of these new transnational regimes—whether the global rights of capital or the human rights of all individuals regardless of nationality. And it is partly because the state has incorporated the objective of furthering a global economy, as is evident in the ascendance of certain government agencies, i.e., the Treasury, and the decline of others, such as those linked to the social fund.

Because so many processes are transnational, governments are increasingly not competent to address some of today's major issues unilaterally or even from the exclusive confines of the inter-state system narrowly defined. This is not the end of state sovereignty; rather the "exclusivity and scope of their competence" has altered, narrowing the range within which the state's authority and legitimacy are operative.

There is no doubt that some of the intellectual technology that governments have and that allow them to exercise control, i.e., Foucault's governmentality, has now shifted to nonstate institutions. This is dramatically illustrated in the new privatized transnational regimes for cross-border business and the growing power of the logic of the global capital market over national economic policy.

These are transformations in the making at this very moment. My reading is that they matter. It is easy to argue the opposite—that the state is still absolute and nothing much has changed. But it may well be the case that these developments signal the beginning of a new era. Scholarship on mentalities has shown how difficult it is for people to recognize systemic change in their contemporary conditions. Seeing continuity is much simpler and often reassuring.

Official immigration policy today is not part of the explicated rules of the new game. Is this helpful in seeking to have a more effective long-term immigration policy in today's globalizing world?

NOTES

1. This paper is based on the author's project *Immigration Policy in a Global Economy: From National Crisis to Multilateral Management*. The broader issues about the state and the global economy are developed in the author's *Losing Control? Sovereignty in an Age of Globalization* (New York: Columbia University Press, 1996).

2. Alongside the well-documented spatial dispersal of economic activities, new forms of territorial centralization of top-level management and control operations have appeared. National and global markets as well as globally integrated operations require central places where the work of globalization gets done. Further, information industries require a vast physical infrastructure containing strategic nodes with hyperconcentrations of facilities. Finally, even the most advanced information industries have a work process—that is, a complex of workers, machines, and buildings that are more place-bound than the imagery of information outputs suggests.

3. Global cities are centers for the *servicing* and *financing* of international trade, investment, and headquarter operations. That is to say, the multiplicity of specialized activities present in global cities are crucial in the valorization, indeed overvalorization of leading sectors of capital today. And in this sense they are strategic production sites for today's leading economic sectors. I have looked at cities as production sites for the leading service industries of our time; one concern was to recover the infrastructure of activities, firms, and jobs that is necessary to run the advanced corporate economy. I focused on the *practice* of global control: the work of producing and reproducing the organization and management of a global production system and a global marketplace for finance.

4. This is a scholarship with a diversity of intellectual lineages. See Sassen, *Losing Control?* for a discussion of this literature as it concerns the particular question under discussion here.

5. Thus, there were centralizing monarchies in Western Europe, city-states in Italy, and city-leagues in Germany. Further, even at a time

when we see the emergence of nation-states with exclusive territoriality and sovereignty, it can be argued that other forms might have become effective alternatives—the Italian city-states, or the Hanseatic League in northern Europe.

6. And its weight in many of the Latin American countries is dubious.

7. For instance, the Universal Declaration was cited in 76 federal cases from 1948 through 1994; over 90 percent of those cases took place since 1980, and of those, 49 percent involved immigration issues, 54 percent if we add refugees. It was also found that the term "human rights" was referred to in 19 federal cases before the twentieth century, 34 times in such cases from 1900 to 1944; 191 times from 1945 to 1969; 803 times in the 1970s; over 2,000 times in the 1980s; and an estimated 4,000 times in the 1990s.

8. There is a whole debate about the notion of citizenship and what it means in the current context. One trend in this debate is a return to notions of cities and citizenship, particularly in so-called global cities, which are partly denationalized territories and have high concentrations of nonnationals from many different parts of the world. The ascendance of human rights codes strengthens these tendencies to move away from nationality and national territory as absolute categories.

9. While these developments are well-known for the cases of Europe and North America, there is not much general awareness of the fact that we are seeing incipient forms in Japan as well. For instance in Japan today we see a strong group of human rights advocates for immigrants, efforts by nonofficial unions to organize undocumented immigrant workers, and organizations working on behalf of immigrants that receive funding from individuals or government institutions in sending countries (e.g., the Thai ambassador to Japan announced in October 1995 that his government will give a total of 2.5 million baht, equivalent to about $100,000, to five civic groups that assist Thai migrant workers, especially undocumented ones; see *Japan Times*, 18 October 1995).

10. Further, the growth of immigration, refugee flows, ethnicity, and regionalism raise questions about the accepted notion of citizenship in

contemporary nation-states and hence about the formal structures for accountability. My research on the international circulation of capital and labor has raised questions for me concerning the meaning of such concepts as national economy and national workforce under conditions of growing internationalization of capital and the growing presence of immigrant workers in major industrial countries. Furthermore, the rise of ethnicity in the United States and in Europe among a mobile workforce raises questions about the content of the concept of nation-based citizenship. The portability of national *identity* raises questions about the bonds with other countries, or localities within them; and the resurgence of ethnic regionalism creates barriers to the political incorporation of new immigrants.

11. There is a large and rich literature on the development of immigration policy at the European level. A bibliography and analyses on the particular angle under discussion here—limitations on the autonomy of the state in making immigration policy—can be found in Sassen, *Losing Control?*

12. Jurisdiction over immigration matters in the U.S. Congress lies with the Judiciary Committee, not with the Foreign Affairs Committee as might have been the case. Congressional intent on immigration is often at odds with the foreign affairs priorities of the Executive. There is a certain policy-making tug-of-war. It has not always been this way. In the late 1940s and 1950s there was great concern with how immigration policy could be used to advance foreign policy objectives. The history of what government agency was responsible for immigration is rather interesting. Earlier, when the Department of Labor (DOL) was created in 1914 it got the responsibility for immigration policy. In June 1933, President Roosevelt combined functions into the Immigration and Naturalization Service within DOL. The advent of World War II brought a shift in the administrative responsibility for the country's immigration policy: in 1940 President Roosevelt recommended it be shifted to the Department of Justice, because of the supposed political threat represented by immigrants from enemy countries. This was meant to last for the extent of the war and then INS supervision was to be returned to the DOL. But it never was. It also meant that immigra-

tion wound up in Congress in committees traditionally reserved for lawyers, as are the Senate and House Judiciary Committees. It has been said that this is why immigration law is so complicated (and, I would add, so centered on the legalities of entry and so unconcerned with broader issues).

13. There are diverse social forces shaping the role of the state depending on the matter at hand. Thus in the early 1980s bank crisis, for instance, the players were few and well coordinated; the state basically relinquished the organizing capacity to the banks, the IMF, and a few other actors. All very discreet, indeed so discreet that if you look closely the government was hardly a player in that crisis. This is quite a contrast with the deliberations around the passing of the 1986 Immigration and Reform Control Act—which was a sort of national brawl. In trade liberalization discussions there are often multiple players, and the executive may or may not relinquish powers to Congress.

14. In this light it is worth noting that in November 1995 a federal judge ruled large sections of Proposition 187 unconstitutional, citing individual rights and the fact that "the state is powerless to enact its own scheme to regulate immigration."

15. The latest study by the Washington-based Urban Institute found that immigrants contribute $30 billion more in taxes than they take in services.

16. President Clinton's 1994 crime bill earmarked $1.8 billion in disbursements over six years to help reimburse states for these incarcerations costs.

17. Increasingly, unilateral policy by a major immigration country is problematic. One of the dramatic examples was that of Germany, which began to receive massive numbers of entrants as the other European states gradually tightened their policies and Germany kept its very liberal asylum policy. Another case is the importance for the EU today that the Mediterranean countries—Italy, Spain, and Portugal—control their borders regarding non-EU entrants.

18. For instance, NAFTA's chapters on services, financial services, telecommunications, and "business persons" contain considerable detail

on the various aspects relating to people operating in a country that is not their country of citizenship. For instance, chapter 12, "Cross-Border Trade in Services," of the NAFTA (White House document, September 29, 1993) includes among its five types of measures those covering "the presence in its territory of a service provider of another Party" under Article 1201, including both provisions for firms and for individual workers. Under that same article there are also clear affirmations that nothing in the agreement on cross-border trade in services imposes any obligation regarding a nonnational seeking access to the employment market of the other country, or to expect any right with respect to employment. Article 1202 contains explicit conditions of treatment of nonnational service providers; so do Articles 1203, 1205, 1210 (especially Annex 1210.5), and 1213.2a and b. Similarly, chapter 13, on telecommunications, and chapter 14, on financial services, contain specific provisions for service providers, including detailed regulations applying to workers. Chapter 16, "Temporary Entry for Business Persons," covers provisions for those "engaged in trade in goods, the provision of services or the conduct of investment activities" (Article 1608).

19. The U.S. delegation for this group is chaired by the Assistant Secretary of State for Consular Affairs and the INS Commissioner.

20. For instance, an item on internal changes in the state that may have impacts on immigration policy is the ascendance of what Charles Keely has called soft security issues. According to some observers, recent government reorganization in the departments of State and Defense, and the CIA reflects an implicit redefinition of national security.

WHAT IS THE PLACE OF
GERMAN CULTURE WITHIN
TODAY'S EUROPEAN CULTURE?

THE FEDERAL REPUBLIC OF GERMANY TURNS FIFTY

Peter Schneider

I would like to begin with a personal note: this year I turned fifty-nine. The birthday child by the name of the Federal Republic of Germany (I'll call him FRG), whom today I will both honor and chide, celebrates his fiftieth. I am, therefore, close to ten years older than the state that grew up next to me. Indeed, due to age differences, I find it difficult to call him my Fatherland. I could already walk and talk before he was even born. And when FRG was finally able to utter a word of German—which was, of course, fashioned mainly by German lawyers—I was already in school learning Latin.

Regardless of where and how we both grew up, the age difference remains. He didn't have an easy childhood and to be sure I didn't always welcome him with open arms. He grew up among disbelieving kids like me and adults who were often much too believing or just submissive. As far as I and a good number of my generation were concerned, we considered this child born in 1949 to be a spin doctor, an impersonator, something like a foreigner. Among his adult guardians, there were many that we knew or at least suspected had earlier just as enthusiastically scored good grades with totally different convictions.

In the 1950s, when I began to reason and FRG learned to walk, we asked ourselves how it could be possible that out of sixty million

Germans not even a few candidates for high public offices could meet one simple qualification: that they had not been a member of the National Socialist German Workers Party. Lübke, Kiesinger, Filbinger, Globke, Chapeau Rouge, and thousands more didn't make it any easier to trust the state's new attire. Thus it came to pass that not a few of us transferred our mistrust of certain individuals to the state and the constitution. In my opinion, the student movement contributed much to the democratization of the Federal Republic. Perhaps its greatest service was that it broke the culture of blind faith in and obedience to the state. God only knows, however, that its goal was not parliamentary democracy. We can only congratulate ourselves and FRG about the fact that we never had the chance to come to power. Such a government would have been not only one of terror, but worse still, one composed of dilettantes. Today one recognizes a thoroughly historical oddity: from the collision of a not-exactly democratic movement with an apathetic and prudish democracy—which in many ways only formally existed—sprang forth one of the most vibrant democracies in the world.

In 1975, when I turned thirty-five and my state turned twenty-six, I had to stand before a court in Berlin and answer questions about my loyalty to the constitution. I had applied for a teaching position in history and German and, because of the new law against "Radicals in Public Service," I was interrogated by the Berlin Education Board about my views. To this very day, I am still proud of the fact that I did not pass my interrogation. I did, however, appeal their decision. The presiding interrogator, a man only slightly older than I, tried to give me a way out and put forth the question: "Mr. Schneider, are you or are you not an enemy of the constitution?" And I, looking into his remarkably blue and truly curious eyes, answered candidly: "Mr. Chairman, I'm not very likely to be an enemy of the constitution. I can't be, for truthfully I read it for the first time only yesterday."

I won the hearing thanks to the presiding judge, who, in addition to his knowledge of the constitution, had a sense of humor. Of course this experience, which, by the way, was a lesson in the independence of justice, got me thinking. Not immediately after my appointment, but rather during the Maoist and terrorist winds that swirled around the student movement, I became—step by step—an ardent friend of the constitution. And I still believe that people like me who from the very beginning questioned everything are better off than most in explaining why democracy is by far the best among all bad forms of government. When asked for the single most important reason why democracy has a better chance of survival in comparison to socialism, I would say that democracy not only tolerates criticism—indeed even radical criticism—but that its very being requires such criticism. Only because of this fundamental openness to discontent and doubt are democracies able to recognize and correct errors and miscalculations in time. In contrast, persecution of doubt and criticism condemns even the most ideal society to collapse under the weight of its unavoidable and irreconcilable errors.

Of course there is no lack of scorn about the fact that a few of society's harshest critics of the Federal Republic now occupy its highest offices. I consider that a good sign. For this process proves the ability of both the system and its critics to change. In short, the relationship between me and that creature nine years younger than I named FRG has relaxed. A generational change and a new cast of characters have made a significant contribution. To be sure, with all the speeches held to commemorate the fiftieth birthday of FRG we must not forget that that day marks only the tenth birthday for the citizens of the former GDR, and that isn't necessarily a reason to celebrate.

Too many of the promises made by big brother have turned out to be hollow; the process of unification was too arrogant and self-confident. Ninety-three percent of the productive capital in the former GDR is now in the hands of West Germans or others, all upper level positions in the administration, judiciary, universities, etc. are filled by West Germans. What is one supposed to think of a rescue team whose lifeboat is filled to the very last seat by its own crew?

Instead of using unification as an opportunity to modernize tired and worn-out concepts found in West German society, these were sim-

ply passed on to the new states without an if, and, or but—the bur-
geoning class of civil servants, the incompetent model of the West
German university, and collective bargaining agreements, just to name
a few of the dinosaurs in the Federal Republic. But even if all these mistakes had not been made, the citizens of the other Germany still would
not have celebrated. By no choice of their own West and East Germans
grew up in radically different boarding schools and both proved to their
respective teachers to be—in good German fashion—exemplary students. According to the absurd measures set out in the law against
"Radicals in Public Office," the West Germans have hundreds of thousands of enemies of the constitution to deal with since the opening of
the East German boarding school. Since I know how long it took me
and others to become friends of the Federal Republic, I would be very
suspicious if this process took place overnight with our colleagues from
the former GDR. Perhaps they must or, at least, should initiate a
"1968" of their own in order to become friends of the constitution. And
once again it will depend on the ability of both sides to renew, both the
challenger as well as the challenged republic, if integration is to be successful. I have little doubt that in the end unification will succeed.

I consider it a blessing that the *querelles allemandes* have been ame-
liorated by the overarching project of European unification. What we
are dealing with here is one of the boldest and noblest plans that this
continent has undertaken in its three-thousand-year history. It is the
first time that a European identity is in the making—a union of states
or a federation?—that is not based on the suppression, conquest, and
pillage of one part by the other, or indeed, as in the National Socialist
version, on the enslavement and annihilation of entire peoples. A
peaceful and voluntary union of a dozen autonomous states would be,
if it succeeds, an utter historical novelty. Every other world power and
empire that we know, from the Imperium Romanum to the British
Empire, from the United States to the former Soviet Union, came into
existence through war.

It is true that Europe is a project of the future—it cannot boast of
a legend about its origins like ancient Athens or the Imperium

Romanum or the Aztec Empire. We have no knowledge of how the divine bull carried the beautiful dark-skinned Europe from the coast of Phoenicia off to the isle of Crete and had three children with her. We know only that his natural playmates, cows, continue to be fed rendered sheep, according to the directives from Brussels, even though they then go mad from it. Today we view the divine abduction and rape of Europe, indeed the first one on the continent, with different eyes. Presumably that clairvoyant bull even then had denounced relations with earthly cows forever.

The question about which marvelous forces will take the place of victorious battles and wars seems already to have been answered: it is the power of money and markets. On one issue it appears that the European managers, the overwhelming majority of whom are orthodox market economists, have revealed themselves to be the last committed Marxists. Apparently they follow the rule that one's economic existence precedes one's conscience and they trust in the fact that from the creation of one common European currency all those other ties that the new union requires will follow.

One is not telling the European Union managers anything new when one maintains that the euro will never earn stability on the stock markets if there is not a new creature that comes into being that uses the euro and calls it his own, namely, the EU-citizen. Or rather, to give him a more pleasant-sounding name, the citizen of Europe. Of course it's not as though the EU managers have not given any thought to this creature. If one compiles all acknowledged data, one can already get an idea about some of his characteristics. Let's take a closer look at Brussels's blueprints of a European.

His most striking characteristic is his strict budgetary discipline. No doubt distinct German characteristics stand out in him. We're talking about a type of person who goes into a panic when his current debt goes over 3 percent of his income and his total debt comprises 60 percent of his annual turnover. He constantly keeps in mind that if he fails he will have enormous penalties to pay or that he will fall back into the ranks of those Europeans who did not make it into the euro elite class.

One already knows what he'll sing to identify himself. As far as a European national anthem goes, a temporary agreement was met only after much fighting back and forth: Beethoven's hymn from the Ninth Symphony is to be the hymn of hope of the new monetary union—to be sure without the accompanying verses that the poet Friedrich Schiller irresponsibly wrote in his mother tongue. I suppose one could translate the words. Of course then we still would be dealing with the translation of a German text that would rouse the sensitivities of our neighbors. "Here was truly a bastard child of the Enlightenment," noted the historian Carl Clark, "a song without words—hope without text."

One sees that the Euro-citizen has little to play with; he is not a Renaissance man. His most significant identity trait—his soul?—is the new banknote that he'll carry around in his wallet. But even the design of the new banknote caused problems. The Euro-engineers were able to agree only that the customary practice of putting the portraits of famous personalities on euro banknotes had to be completely done away with. As far as using the likeness of politicians goes, one can understand the concern: Napoleon awakens utterly different memories in France than in Germany or England. The same goes for Frederick the Great, Bismarck, or Churchill. But what could be the problem with the impressive ancestral gallery of those free and multilingual souls who lived and created long before there were nation-states: Copernicus, Spinoza, Galileo Galilei, Michelangelo, Leonardo da Vinci, Rembrandt, Voltaire, Alexander von Humboldt, Goethe, Mozart, Bettina von Arnim, Chopin, Chechov, Brecht, Thomas Mann, Marie Curie, Else Lasker-Schüler, Camus, Hannah Arendt, Einstein? They all have one defect in common: in the meantime they all (and not seldom unjustly) have been made representatives of a certain nation and, there-fore, could injure the feelings of their neighbors. For this reason, the Eurocrats could only bring themselves to agree on the least common denominator: not persons, but rather buildings, or more accurately, architectural elements connoting union, are to support the new cur-rency—arches, gateways, and bridges.

Here a paradox of the European union under the scepter of the euro becomes clear. Precisely that which defines European character, namely the diversity of her culture, the Euro-managers want to abolish in favor of a cantankerously settled community. There are neither myths nor concepts behind the cultural and moral affiliations in this cultural community. As far as the definition of the Euro-banana or Euro-apple, however, one is not left in the dark. The standard EU-banana, for example, must be 27 mm in diameter, "measured in the center section of the fruit between either side of the longitudinal axis," and the length "must be at least 14 cm measured from the tip of the banana to the outer arch to the end of the stem." Won't we then be held liable to find Euro-norms similar to those of the Euro-banana for those crops that don't grow in fields, say, for example, Europe's intellectual products? Will there be a Euro-liberty? A Euro-equality? A Euro-human? And weren't we already treating those groups and races that do not meet or who refuse these norms like those fish that do not measure up and, thus, get tossed back into the sea?

What language will the Euro-human speak? It is not easy to understand the European hesitation in promoting a common language for the dominion of the new currency. Apparently the Euro-managers are having a hard time recognizing that there has long been a European lingua franca. To be sure it is not the language of Goethe, nor that of Voltaire, nor even that of Dante. No, it is the language of McDonald's, Disneyland, Michael Jordan, and Leonardo DiCaprio, but also the language of Shakespeare, Newton, Edgar Allan Poe, William Faulkner, James Joyce, and Bob Dylan. Europe can live with that.

As it stands, the citizens of Europe will have a common currency beginning in 2002, but I fear that as far as a common mode of communication is concerned, the majority will still have to rely on sign language, an area where the Italians clearly have an advantage.

The European lingua franca will mostly be one's second language and will never replace the respective mother tongue. For this reason alone, an entirely different form of diversity can and will develop in Europe than did in the United States. Seen from a European perspective, the "cultural mix" in the United States seems in many ways to be an American brand of a cultural mix, if not an illusion. Each person, no matter where he comes from, must first adopt the American language and culture before he can celebrate his much-acclaimed cultural differences. A European wonders why the heroes in a Hollywood film have no difficulty understanding one another—no matter where they come from. Whether a Sioux Indian chief, someone from Greenland, or a Vietnamese guerilla, they all speak with the appropriate American accent. In Europe and elsewhere, successful films can only make it in America when they go through an American remake with American sets and American actors. Europe would be able to follow this example only at the expense of self-sacrifice. I've heard that since the recent merger of Chrysler-Daimler the following rule applies at the main office in Stuttgart: if one single manager from the United States is present, then everybody must speak English. I am not exactly known as a defender of German national concerns, but I do love my language. Is it too much to ask of two companies that join forces that they show deference to the respective languages and cultures they represent? Recognizing a foreign language means a lot more than simply recognizing a different system of phonetics and a different grammar. It requires recognizing different traditions, other views of history and the world. The assertion that there is such a thing as a European culture that is somehow different from an American, African, Arabic, or Asian one cannot be disputed. Under dispute is solely the question of what the noteworthy characteristics of this culture are.

Ten years ago I labeled Europe the "culture of doubt" and expressed hope that shades of doubt might have a chance to become historically significant. "It is as plain as day," I wrote at the time, "that doubt thrives best where different thought, speech and life patterns collide with one another without any one in particular having the power to set itself apart as the only true one." In the meantime I've come to have my doubts about this definition. Today all talk is, I fear, not about European culture, but rather about one simple endangered thing, namely, the indispensable preconditions of culture, not just the European one. To these preconditions belongs the resolute defense against barbarism—destroying aspirations, among which I count attacks on racial or religious minorities, calculated expulsion, mass rape, mass murder of such minorities, the construction of concentration camps, and tolerance of racial hatred.

What does it mean when a culture—as happened during the Bosnian war—no longer views the outbreak of barbaric acts in its midst as a threat, but rather declares it as something foreign, a Balkan specialty? Indeed it means that this culture has forgotten that it arose—perhaps not all too long ago—from the conscious effort and suppression of such culture, from destroying energies that it now looks upon helplessly and that it doesn't want to recognize again. The war in Bosnia and now in Kosovo has reminded us that culture is not something that we have by nature, something that belongs to us forever, but rather that it is highly fragile, and based on an agreement that is constantly threatened and in need of constant renewal and redesign.

The West and also the Germans have learned from the trauma wrought by helplessly looking on through years of murder and expulsion in Bosnia. NATO has come through on its threat to protect the most elementary human rights—even to the point of a military intervention—and has shown those persecuted and scorned in Kosovo that there is someone in the world that is at least willing not to stand by and watch barbaric deeds be carried out. This act of intervention should not be underestimated. At the same time it has been clear for weeks that the continued bombardment of Yugoslavia has missed its most important goal. Not only has it not hindered the expulsion of one and a half million people, but it has also hastened these misdeeds. How can it be explained that the most powerful military force in the world was incapable of taking control of an area not much larger than Los Angeles and protecting its population from murder and expulsion? I fear the answer is terribly simple: each and every resolute dictator can defy even the most powerful military machine in the world if he has reason to believe that the readiness of that military to employ its might has a condition—that is, the intervention may, in principle, not cost the life of one single soldier.

In the meantime, the war in Kosovo has forced Germans to change their perception of themselves and their understanding of history from the bottom up. In contrast to their engagement in Bosnia, this time they are more than symbolically present—suddenly the rules of the game are changing. Was it not a rather peculiar, even an eerie point, many ask, that a kind of privilege could be deduced from the insight into Germany's historical guilt. In the case of Bosnia most Germans agreed that young Swedes, Danes, Frenchmen, Americans, and the Dutch ought to risk their necks for human rights. But out of consideration of their Nazi past, such actions should never be expected of the Germans?

The consensus "war, never again" that was until recently undisputed, now proves to be incomplete. True, it is historically understandable and highly desirable to the world, but at the same time it turns out to be insufficient: it is a lesson that indeed could be popular only in the land of the aggressor.

For we now suddenly realize that the peoples who were overrun by the German Nazis could not draw the same conclusion from their past. They had to take to arms in order to free themselves from the Nazi barbarians. Should not the slogan have read: "Never again aggression. Never again genocide"? And are the political and moral themes that follow from this teaching still the same as the ones that were valid before? Kosovo is not Auschwitz, as we have heard, and we agree. But isn't there something false when the acknowledgment of the uniqueness of German guilt becomes an excuse for Germans not to intervene against mass murder and ethnic cleansing in Bosnia or in Kosovo?

If Auschwitz is to be the measure, then we'll never need to intervene anywhere in the world, for none of the present day crimes measures up to Auschwitz. All at once, the question as to the correct lesson from Germany's past is newly formulated.

So, you can see that, after all, FRG and I are on speaking terms. But there is still something I cannot cope with. Although FRG is quite well behaved, internationally respected, and sometimes even liked, he is in a strange way immovable, full of "Angst"—he is, to say the least, not a risk taker. Why? For historic reasons Germany could be—and in many ways is—one of the most dynamic and modern societies in Europe, for almost every tradition had to be examined for the Nazi virus and not a few traditions were turned upside down. But sometimes it seems to me that FRG has abolished some of the good traditions along with the bad.

On a recent evening in what was once East Berlin, I received a sign from the heavens. Where once a famous socialist fish restaurant had advertised its "Dinner from the Sea"—in an unforgettable neon blue light—I discovered a new message: "Pioneer." After a while I realized it was just a new company name, but for a second it seemed that that neon sign inscribed in the evening sky was a manifestation of something whose absence was overwhelming, and an almost forbidden thought came to my mind. Where is the pioneering spirit? What happened to the courage of the Germans, their intrepidness, their spirit of discovery and invention, the endless desire to create what Goethe was so proud of? Have they forgotten that they brought forth scientific explorers like Alexander von Humboldt and so many sons and daughters who helped build that "land of the future," the United States of America?

Anyone who takes on an enormous task—and the unification of two formerly divided states and their integration into the formerly divided Europe is an enormous task—must be willing to take risks. It doesn't need pride or megalomania, but something far simpler, which may be the most difficult thing of all for Germans. It requires a willingness to put into play a sense of beauty and at least a tolerable amount of self-love. After all, if you can't love yourself, you can't love someone else.

Translated by Frank Wagner

THE HUMBOLDT-GOETHE COMPLEX

Helmut Müller-Sievers

It is only since the early nineteenth century that language and culture have been compared to living organisms. This comparison has been of paramount importance to modern German history. It allowed for the claim to individuality and identity, for only organisms embody the principle of individuality, and it allowed for the claim to a proper history, for only organisms can have a past and a future. This last point, which informs our discussion today, is worth repeating: only organisms have a past and a future of their own. If language is conceived as a logical form, like French in the seventeenth and eighteenth centuries, it can attain only differing degrees of perfection; if it is conceived as an inventory of all possible ideas, as Chinese language and script, it can attain only differing degrees of completion; or if it is conceived as a present of God, as Hebrew, it can attain only differing degrees of disclosure. In none of these cases can one properly speak of a life, a history, and thus of a future of a language and, along with it, of the culture in which it is embedded.

The idea that language and culture are best understood as mutually fertilizing organisms found powerful expression in Wilhelm von Humboldt's philosophy of language. Although Humboldt had cosmopolitan interests and liberal political views, his philosophy entailed a hierarchical typology of languages. If it were language's task to represent the absolute motility of the human spirit, then the language that provided the highest degree of articulation and the highest condensation of meaningful elements would naturally be superior. Of course, no language represents spirit perfectly, but some come closer than others do. Sanskrit, for example, allows for a higher degree of freedom in its word order and has more signifying elements than any living language; ancient Greek is almost as rich, and among the living languages it seems to be German that comes closest to the expression of spirit. Turkish, to use an example of unexpected actuality, unnecessarily weighs down free expression by its practice of agglutination, of gluing together elements rather than condensing them meaningfully. This hierarchy of articulation overshadows Humboldt's otherwise unprejudiced investigation into world languages.

Organisms are animated phenomena. The spirit that animates the organism of German language and culture has had various names in the nineteenth and twentieth centuries, from *Bildungskraft* to *Weltgeist* to *Volksgeist*. Whatever its name, there always remains a rest that cannot be fully and logically explained. One needs to be part of the organism, or at least have access to it through empathy, in order to grasp its essence. This ineffability of the spirit is what remained of God in modernity. Because of this spiritual residue, the idea of organicity always carries a strong moral connotation: organic phenomena are good and organization is desirable; mechanistic phenomena are deficient and anachronistic. The greatest exponent of organic thought in Germany was, of course, Goethe. His oeuvre contains substantial works directly concerned with the theory of organisms; more importantly, however, he understood his own artistic development as an organic process. In his autobiographic writings, Goethe indicated—some have said dictated—to his future readers how he should be understood: as an organic part of a culture that he has helped to shape. From this follows an empathetic theory of interpretation: just as there is always an ineffable residue in organic phenomena, so there is in works of literature a spiritual remnant that can only be divined or felt. Literary criticism and linguistic competence are thus ultimately tied to a sense of belonging that can only be acquired with great difficulty.

Wilhelm von Humboldt founded the high schools and universities in which his organicist linguistics and the literature of his friend Goethe were first taught. A prolonged exposure to the study of languages and to the works of ancient and national authors, culminating in the works of Goethe, became the precondition for membership in the social and cultural elites, the German *Buildingsbürgertum*. This close interaction between a politician who was a philosopher and dabbling poet, and a poet who was a philosopher and a dabbling politician, is unique in Europe, and its consequences can be felt until today. Every general debate about education, about the state of public culture and language in Germany, before and after reunification, is set in the frame marked by Humboldt and Goethe.

I submit that the Humboldt-Goethe complex, much like the military-industrial complex in this country, has been a misfortune for German language and culture. The idea that language and culture, politics and poetics should be related in an organic way has created an expectation of harmony and a blindness to the necessity and permanence of conflict. Emulating Goethe's, and to a lesser degree Humboldt's, disgust for dissidence, the institutions of higher learning and the fora of public opinion still manage to exclude and stifle most expressions of fundamental criticism. It is startling to realize that among the hundreds of scholarly books and articles written each year on Goethe (and what is called the *Goethe-Zeit*) there are perhaps not more than a handful that could be called critical, even in the most rudimentary sense of scrutinizing whether the author's professed intentions represent really the ultimate wisdom of interpretation. And if someone were to write such critical books and articles, I think it's not too paranoid to assume that she would find it very difficult to find a position in today's German university.

It is equally startling to realize to what degree contemporary German literature, and the popular taste for cultural products, has been bound by the Goethean paradigm. By that I mean the trust in conventional forms of narration, in the pedagogical and political relevance of literature and art, and in the elevation of the author beyond the realm of craft and artistic accountability. I realize that I am generalizing here, but I think a dispassionate comparison of, say, German, French, and American literature in the last fifty years would show how uninterested the Germans were, and are, in formal innovation and in the autonomy of fictional and artistic content.

Current debates over cultural identity in reunited Germany rely heavily on Goethean metaphors of cultural organicity. After having been separated "artificially" by an unnatural barrier, the two halves now have to "grow together" again, and they can do this all the more easily because they are nourished by the same "humanistic," i.e., Goethean, essence. As an overview over this year's festivities (of which we are a part) clearly shows, the importance of Goethe as the integrating figure, and of Weimar as the cultural capital, simply cannot be overestimated. I must repeat that from the outside this valorization and heroization of a poet looks odd and slightly troublesome. It is not always clear whether the passages from Goethe's works quoted at such occasions are understood as what they are, namely words of an eighteenth-century poet, and not as directives for the government of a twentieth-century state.

It must also be said—and here I know I can except present company—that the debates among intellectuals in Germany, before and after the fall of the Wall, are often characterized by an extraordinary desire for historical harmony and reconciliation, by a diffuse resentment for the injustices of the world, and by a filial disappointment in the agencies of the state. Of course, this has everything to do with the relations between the generations and the failure of the older generation to acknowledge their involvement in the atrocities of the Nazi state. And yet it is startling to observe the slow awakening of German intellectuals from the dream of historical harmony, unilinear progress, and ultimate reconciliation of all contradictions.

Nothing I have said so far constitutes a negative judgment of Goethe's poetical prowess; in fact, if one abstracts from the endless diaries and self-reflections and conversations in which he himself becomes caught up in his own image as a prophet and sage, Goethe might turn out to be a much more interesting and complicated writer than his admirers want to admit. I have been circumscribing the unbroken predominance of an aesthetic ideology in which Goethe's name functions as a cipher, as a trope that means different things to different people and something for everybody. The question remains whether there is any trait in Goethe's oeuvre that qualifies him for this position, or whether it was really only the historical contigency of the emergence of the German nation-state and its need for identity. I think there is such a trait, and Goethe himself has confessed to it as a weakness: it is his inability to think and write tragically. In a letter to Schiller he wrote: "I don't know myself well enough to say whether I would be able to write a true tragedy, but I tremble at the thought of such an undertaking and am convinced that the mere attempt would destroy me" (Ich kenne mich zwar nicht selbst genug um zu wissen, ob ich eine wahre Tragödie schreiben könnte, ich erschrecke aber blos vor dem Unternehmen und bin beynahe überzeugt daß ich mich durch den bloßen Versuch zerstören könnte. [To Schiller, 12/9/1797]). This avoidance of tragedy characterizes the entirety of Goethe's works and it is, I think, the secret of his cooptation as the *spiritus rector* of German culture and language. Goethe clings to the belief that all contradictions can be resolved, that all antagonisms can be reconciled, that all opposition will find a common ground. Even in his bleakest works there is always a substantial ray of hope, a reassurance that no conflict is unavoidable, that even where humans fail there will be some form of providence to rescue them.

This untragic vision is at the heart of Goethe's philosophy of organisms and of his understanding of the history of culture and language. In natural organisms the opposition of matter and spirit is resolved in the concepts of growth and metamorphosis, the opposition between individual and community is resolved and sublated in the organism of culture, and the conflict between intention and convention finds a solution in the organism of language. The organicist view of continuous growth also implies that every present conflict will find its solution in the future and that, in this sense, the present is nothing but a prelude. These twin tendencies of reconciliation and futurity have recommended Goethe's oeuvre (rather than, say, Kleist's or Hoelderlin's) for the political and ideological parts it has been playing since the early nineteenth century. And in return, they have shaped German public debates in the way I have tried to outline above.

I want to make sure that the call for a more tragic vision of culture and history implied in my critique is not misunderstood as political acquiescence or passivity. None of the national myths that have so disastrously motivated German politics in the last two centuries qualify as tragedies, nor do the bellicose and ultimately genocidal actions they have helped to motivate. I also don't mean by tragic vision the mumblings of a Syberberg or a Botho Strauss who, once again, confuse tragedy with destiny or *Schicksal*. I simply mean the recognition that some, maybe even a great many, contradictions in cultural life cannot be resolved and that precisely because of this insight they require active and careful political intervention.

Of course, there is no question that German language and culture will have a future even if the Goethean avoidance of tragedy is retained as the overarching cultural paradigm, as most events this year seem to indicate. It will be a future in which conflicts are solved in the usual way of either integrating or excluding the conflictual elements and debating where the limits should be. It will be a future that very much resembles the past and the present and therefore not much of a future, a *Zukunft*, at all. If, however, the Goethean paradigm of organic integration, its thirst for reconciliation, and its aesthetics of harmony are abandoned, a different future could begin. Its guiding question would not be how to integrate foreign elements but how to keep their conflicts productive. Language would no longer be perceived as an organic patrimony in need of conservation and regulation by state laws, but as a multiplicity of more or less stable dialects that might, or might not, exchange their vocabulary. Literature could shake the imperative of first having to communicate or contribute something to current debates and then concentrate on questions of form and medium. The debates about the cultural future of Germany, finally, could move away from the obsession with integrating some disparate elements and expelling others, and ask which conflicts it can bear and which conflicts threaten to undermine the very possibility of conflict.

"We are one people," as the demonstrators shouted ten years ago, might have been a good political slogan at the time, but it makes for a boring and ultimately stifling cultural vision. Lionel Trilling once said that human intelligence is measured according to how many contrary convictions a mind can accommodate. Similarly, cultural intelligence might be measured according to the degree of variety or, if you forgive the coinage, how much disparation it is able to endure. It is only in such variety and disparation that one can see a future.

HOW DIVERSE IS THE GERMAN CULTURAL MARKET?

RESHUFFLING THE DECK: DEMOCRATIZATION AND DIVERSIFICATION OF THE CULTURAL MARKET

Henryk Broder

Speaking about Germany—it's a difficult task, a thankless job. Either you cater to expectations or you disappoint your public. Since 1945 Germany is a huge open air lab with some seventy to eighty million guinea pigs under control and observation. Everything is being watched: what they do, what they don't do, how they act and react, how they grow and develop. Being German is something no reasonable person would voluntarily opt for.

Because being German means you have always to decide: do you take the wrong way or do you take the false way? Because there is simply no right way to go. If you are against the war, if you are a pacifist, then you are a coward and you did not learn the lesson of history. However: if you are for the war, you are not simply a warmonger, you want to continue the imperialist-militarist German tradition—and you did not learn the lesson of history either. So you try to find a convenient compromise: you are basically against the war but for a limited military intervention. Or you are for the war but against sending ground troops. You try to end up on the right side of the fence whatever you decide to do.

But being German is also something very rewarding. Especially being a German Jew or a Jew residing in Germany. There are dozens of

German-Jewish dialogue groups, even in the United States, sponsored by churches, political parties, and foundations, all of them trying to "normalize" German-Jewish relations. I always wonder what the dialogue is about: how to prepare gefilte fish and serve it as Bismarck herring? Or how to find a Jewish spouse without converting to Judaism? There is no such thing as a German-Italian or German-Bulgarian dialogue. But there is an ongoing German-Jewish dialogue. And, unlike *Seinfeld*, which is a show about nothing, this dialogue is about something. But what is it? I guess it gives both sides the opportunity to continue performing the roles of victims and villains, only the roles are reversed. Now the Germans are the victims, they suffer and they repent, while the Jews enjoy being on the top, having an upper hand, being morally superior. What a great experience after two thousand years of discrimination. And now the Jews are helping the Germans to come to terms with their past. Like Daniel Libeskind, they are building Jewish museums; like Peter Eisenman, they are designing Holocaust memorials; and, like me, they are writing articles about why Jews should not interfere with German affairs, thus becoming part of the dialogue but on a much higher intellectual level.

And there is something else you may consider to be typically German: evade your subject, never talk about a topic you are supposed to talk about. That's exactly what I am doing now. But, on the other hand, this attitude can also be seen as democratization and diversification of culture. Let me explain what I mean: Germany is undergoing tremendous changes and while many Germans are afraid that Germany is changing for the worse, I am sure that Germany is changing for the better. Maybe not in terms of the economy, technical standards, and political weight, but in terms of pluralism, liveliness, food, entertainment, and general mood. Some concerned Germans call it the Americanization of Germany—and they are right! No other state, no other society in Europe resembles the United States as much as Germany. With two major differences: we do not have capital punishment—which is good—and we do not have a speed limit on the Autobahn—which is bad. Because having no speed limit is our substitute for capital punishment.

Germany is in fact becoming a multicultural, multiethnic, multi-religious society. The only problem is: many Germans haven't gotten it yet, and those who have gotten it start feeling like foreigners in their own home (Schoenbohm in Berlin). In big cities like Cologne, Frankfurt, Stuttgart, and Berlin the so-called foreigners amount to 15, 20, even 25 percent of the population. And while they were almost invisible twenty years ago, they are now becoming very much visible. All of a sudden there is a black waiter at my favorite café, the Montevideo on Victoria Luise Platz, and his German is as good as mine. I must admit: the first time I saw him I was surprised; now I take it for granted that my doctor's assistant is from India, the guy at my bank is from England, and my photo editor at *Der Spiegel* was born in Romania.

Germany is simply becoming less German, except for the *Neue Bundesländer*, the new territories in the East, the former GDR, where you have very few foreigners (less than 1 percent), but much more hatred against foreigners—that includes also Germans from the West—than in other parts of Germany. But it is only a matter of time, maybe twenty, maybe thirty years, until the Easterners catch up with the West and stop chasing and beating people, just for fun, who happen to be dark-skinned or speak with a foreign accent. For the time being that is reason enough in cities like Cottbus and Brandenburg to stay at home after sunset.

But, I have to emphasize, Germany has recently changed its laws of citizenship. Kids of immigrants can now become German citizens if they wish to. And that's a big step forward toward a civic society and a democratic culture. A Moslem of Turkish origin, a black whose parents came from Africa, a Vietnamese descendant of boat people will carry German passports. It's hard to believe but it's true. It all began not in 1968, as is widely believed, but in 1989 when the Berlin Wall came down and history returned to Germany. Reunification was a windfall benefit—the Germans were taken by surprise, especially the citizens of the Federal Republic. Leftist intellectuals were shocked, even traumatized. First because something had happened that they had not foreseen and secondly because they were not asked for permission and advice.

Tucholsky would say: "Sie sassen in der Ecke und nahmen übel"

(They retreated into a corner and were holding a grudge against the rest of the world). Usually smart and decent minds like Günter Grass were running berserk. Even after the collapse of the GDR, when things became irreversible, he kept complaining about that tragic error of history. He really took it to heart. He felt abused. His main argument was that because of Auschwitz Germany must not become a unified sovereign state. And he called the GDR "eine kommode Diktatur" (a comfortable, cozy dictatorship). Others wanted the communist experiment, which they were watching from a safe distance, to continue until final victory. And others were afraid of a Fourth Reich. This was wishful thinking of the naive left: if a Fourth Reich would come up they would prove that they could do what their parents failed to do—resist and fight! Of course, they would not. But they enjoyed this daymare fantasy like kids dreaming of becoming Robin Hood before they wake up.

I knew better. I knew that Germany would become bigger but not stronger—that it would, in fact, become weaker. The only question I was asking myself and my friends was: would we spoil them with democracy or would they rather contaminate us with their acquired habits, their love for rituals, desire for security, contempt for the individual, and need for leadership? And that is still a pending question (Schily, Limbach, Gauck).

Unification has indeed changed the fabric of German society even though people in Cologne, Trier, and Saarbruecken continue to live as if nothing has happened. "Die Karten wurden neu gemischt" (the deck has been reshuffled): that means not only that seventeen million people in the old East can now participate in democracy (and many of them probably enjoy it), but also that in the old West a new dynamic is changing the traditional terms of power. Important people are now less important and former nobodies get a chance to show their talents. Big shots like Günter Grass, Christa Wolf, or Walter Jens who served as moral institutions, heroes, icons, and role models have been reduced to their real size and they are not too happy about it. During the Gulf War they were producing resolutions and declarations on an assembly line.

Walter Jens was even hiding two U.S. soldiers in his house, torturing them with the food his wife was cooking. To score points in a more public fashion he informed press agencies about his contribution to end the war against Saddam Hussein. Now, during the war against Milosevic, most of the big minds have kept a low profile. The most courageous intervention came from the desk of Christoph Hein, the new president of the German PEN club. He suggested that German television should stop showing entertaining programs as long as the war is going on. But no one listened to him.

These are good signs. And in spite of all the pessimistic forecasts, more books are written, published, and sold then ever before and there are more jobs for writers, editors, and directors because three dozen TV stations need lots of material. I have found it very pleasing and comforting that the Grand Prix d'Eurovison, the European Song Contest, is as important an event as any literary festival, that the question of who is going to represent us in this contest excites millions of people who are not normally considered consumers of culture. Last year I was torn between my two loyalties: Israel was represented in this contest by Dana International, a wonderful, sexy transvestite, and Germany by a singer named Guildo Horn whose special shtick is to make fun of show business. In the end I was delighted: the Germans gave their votes to Dana International and the Israelis, who really understand and appreciate crazy behavior, voted for Guildo Horn. Under these circumstances it is a tough job, almost mission impossible, to attract attention within the limits of the conventional cultural market. And one has to work very hard to make people angry and to trigger a public discussion—like Martin Walser, whose political views were subject to frequent changes, or Peter Handke, who used to be an angry young man and is now an aging Austrian *Grantler,* someone who loves to be in a bad mood.

Martin Walser, as you may know, gave a speech last year saying that he was fed up with the Holocaust stuff he is being forced to watch on TV. He can't take it anymore. And Peter Handke went to Belgrade and took sides with Mr. Milosevic, the innocent victim of fascist aggression.

Handke claimed that NATO is doing to the Serbs what the Nazis were doing to the Jews. But these are minor events in the political and cultural context of the new Germany, second-rate sensations, good enough to stir up some controversy and promote public discussions with the usual suspects as participants. But not strong enough to move the clock back.

And that's really good news from Germany today.

BEYOND GOETHE: PERSPECTIVES ON POSTUNIFICATION GERMAN LITERATURE

Dagmar C. G. Lorenz

Today's leading German magazines and newspapers have a global per-spective: the crisis in Kosovo, elections in Israel and their impact on the Middle Eastern peace process, and millennial concerns make headlines there as they do in the United States. In addition, events pertaining to German history are being especially chronicled this year, which marks not only the two-hundred-and-fiftieth anniversary of Goethe's birth, but also the fiftieth anniversary of the Federal Republic of Germany, to whose history *Der Spiegel* has devoted an extensive, ongoing series en-titled *50 Jahre Bundesrepublik: Das deutscheWunder* (50 Years of the Federal Republic of Germany: The German Miracle).[1] The special issue calls for reconsideration of issues such as German nationhood, not without, to be sure, manipulation of historical facts. After all, according to Walter Benjamin it is the victors who write the history,[2] and West Germany has won the Cold War. Over the course of more than a hundred pages the *Spiegel* issue covers the following topics: "The Years of Hunger," "The Adenauer Era," "The Era after Adenauer," "The Brandt Era," "The Schmidt Era," "The Kohl Era." After German unification, West German history is all that remains. Clearly, a merger has not taken place between East and West, but rather a takeover. However, the Federal Republic's history is overshadowed by the Nazi past of which critical journalists such as Henryk Broder do not tire of reminding the public.[3] As far as the former GDR, East Germany, is concerned, little positive is remembered in the media. Government abuses and social ills are foregrounded and new revelations about the activities of the Stasi, East Germany's infamous secret police, are brought to light.[4] It is obvious that the integration of East and West has not yet been completed. No less than the revision of German citizenship laws and the status of foreign workers and other immigrants, the legacy of the GDR is part of Germany's multicultural landscape.

All discussion of Germany's recent past takes place in the shadow of that of the "most recent past," a term that continues to be understood as a reference to the Nazi era and the Holocaust. There is the ongoing struggle concerning restitution for slave laborers against unwilling German industrial concerns, the debate over the Holocaust memorial in Berlin, the suit against the Dresdner Bank, a major financial backer of the SS,[5] the debate over a German military cemetery at Stalingrad,[6] and continued scrutiny of the attitude of politicians toward the Nazi past, even if or particularly since many of them were, like Chancellor Gerhard Schröder, still in diapers, as David Hudson noted in the *Spiegel*: "A new generation is at the helm, playing host this week to the U.S. president and to the leaders of the G-8 nations as they forged a proposal for peace in Kosovo. Nevertheless, this new generation must carry on with the business of settling accounts between Germany and its victims during the war, though for millions, of course, there will never be exculpation."[7] What, if any, role can German-language literature play in Europe and Germany at the end of the twentieth century, when aesthetic pursuits and criticism are the privilege of a select few?

Literature has traditionally played a significant role in shaping national discourses, for example in Austria after the Napoleonic occupation, in the GDR, where the great German heritage of Goethe, Schiller, and the nineteenth century was embraced, and in the Federal Republic, where the *Kahlschlag* or the Point Zero, proclaimed in the postwar era, called for a distancing from tradition, including the Nazi legacy. Cultural production and politics are linked and take place on a global scale, as is obvious in the controversy about the Holocaust memorial and the current discussions on issues concerning gender and power, which run parallel to similar discussions in the U.S. media. In Germany there is an increasing awareness of the importance of gender in the sphere of high culture, as is clear in the current exhibit "Zwischen Ideal und Wirklichkeit" in Gotha, featuring women's painting and sculpture from the age of Goethe, which has been extensively discussed in *Die Welt*.[8] In German commercial culture, particularly advertisement, a similar awareness has not yet been developed, as images promoting cars, clothes, and furniture illustrate. Culture and politics also converge in the reassessment of Holocaust writers such as George Tabori,[9] as well as in the outrage over Binjamin Wilkomirski's inauthentic autobiography entitled *Bruchstücke. Eine Kindheit 1939– 1948*, revealing a continuum between past and present.[10] So do discussions of the conflict in the Balkans in light of World War II. History looms large in Hans Peter Schwarz's review *Nie war sie so wertvoll wie heute. Die Geschichte der Bundesrepublik in zwei Essaybänden*, which discusses the concepts of the nation-state and national identity in the context of post-Shoah Germany.[11]

While immigrants and refugees enter postunification Germany, citizenship laws are revised and nationhood, nation-state, and national identity are burning issues once again. It is apparent that the nineteenth-century model of the nation-state (at that time a new model) no longer applies to the new realities. Today's united Germany is a political entity without precedence. In the age of Goethe, kindled by the French Revolution and the Napoleonic occupation, nation, nationality, and nationhood were debated and a united Germany was envisioned as an ideal. This ideal prevailed against the older dynastic model. Johann Wolfgang von Goethe, court poet and court politician, like the Jewish writer Heinrich Heine and the Austrian author Franz Grillparzer, was suspicious of the young German nationalists, the *Deutschtümler*, and events proved him right, including the 1819 attacks on Jewish neighborhoods and ghettos.

To this day Goethe, among other things, is heralded as the proponent of a supranational European ideal. Goethe, the poet, critic, politician, genius, and world-citizen, has become something like a brand name. The Deutsche Welle devotes its *Goethe Bytes* to him, which are designed to show Goethe's significance and influence.[12] Goethe—what German high school graduate would not know at least one of his poems, "Heidenröslein" or "Erlkönig," or the tragic König von Thule, who died of a broken heart? Or some of the exuberant literary characters created by Goethe with whom the author himself is often confused—Werther and Faust, and why not Iphigenie, the mouthpiece of universal tolerance and intercultural understanding? Goethe had already become a monument in his lifetime, and his home the site of secular pilgrimages. During the Nazi era countless exiles and concentration camp prisoners considered Goethe a symbol of the "good" Germany, their legitimate connection with German culture.

Remaining a relatively uncontroversial German (compared to Heine, Nietzsche, Wagner, Brecht), Goethe has remained something like a model character for observers who are taken aback by the nationalist and xenophobic currents in unified Germany as well as for those who champion a united Europe. There are, in fact, good reasons for commemorating Goethe, who distrusted the awakening German nationalism as much as he abhorred the bloodshed of the French Revolution, who was apprehensive of the excesses of the mind he perceived in Romanticism and critical of unchecked technological progress, who opposed the mechanistic view of the universe, including one of its major exponents, Isaac Newton, and who pleaded for an enlightened, humane way of dealing with social problems such as single motherhood.

But how German is Goethe? Germany in the sense of 1871 did not exist at the time Goethe grew up in Frankfurt and in the years when he served at the court of Weimar. Even if it had, how typical a representative of such a Germany would Goethe have been? According to Dan Wilson's recent critical Goethe study, the traditional image of Goethe as humanist and forward-looking social thinker and politician needs to be thoroughly revised as well.[13]

Leaving aside his prodigious talents, Goethe was the product of a small segment of German society: a male child born into a privileged upwardly mobile stratum of a hierarchical social order. Few speakers of German were so fortunate to have private tutors, study foreign languages, become introduced to cutting-edge science and philosophy. The Jewish-born novelist and critic Fanny Lewald compares Goethe's career to that of a likewise bright, likewise ambitious young man, Loeb Baruch, later Ludwig Börne. She wonders what would have become of the latter had he not been raised locked up in the overpopulated Frankfurt ghetto, which nobody was allowed to leave even under dire circumstances such as fire emergencies.[14] It is pointless to ask what might have become of Goethe had he been born into different circumstances: Goethe was who he was, including his birth, his position, his privileges upon all of which rests his literary production.

When contemplating Goethe and his era, it is important to remember that Germany was not yet associated with the Holocaust and the attempts to exterminate human beings considered unfit to be German. The population of the German-speaking states was relatively homogeneous, mobility low, and the great liberation movements of the nineteenth century were just about to begin—those of the Jews, women, and the working class.

Goethe did not champion German superiority when many of his younger contemporaries did. Rooted in the Enlightenment, his writings show greater compassion than those of the following generations, such as Fichte, Hebbel, and Wagner. But of course, Goethe shared many of the views and biases of his contemporaries. Therefore neither his nor his era's legacy can possibly be considered models for the millennium to come. To meet the challenges of the present age, Europe needs to reinvent itself from the bottom up. This includes finding modes of communication and literary expressions that reach beyond the confines of high culture and involve more than just the nations that have traditionally assumed leadership roles in matters of economics and culture (and in this precise order). Cultural achievements and patterns that depend so clearly on inequality, on the discrimination and exploitation of vast segments of the population as did those at the age of Goethe, fostering the very elitism that became synonymous with German education are not viable models for a future German culture in the larger European context.

Goethe's universalism and humanism are objects of highest praise. Yet, which strata of German society were truly touched by these lofty ideals influence outside of the Humanistische Gymnasien and universities, these traditionally classist, nationalist, sexist, and anti-Semitic flagships of German education throughout the nineteenth and into the twentieth century? Exclusionary in policy and function, they were never intended to bring the optimal amount of education to the largest number of students. Rather, they were regulators of language, cultural codes, and ideas. The traditional three-tiered educational system reinforced established class barriers. Already the grammatical and mathematical terminology taught in the lower-level Volks- and Mittelschule signaled class-belonging and status among speakers of German within a five-minute conversation; so did the knowledge of classical mythology and languages taught exclusively at the Gymnasium. In other words, Goethe's linguistic code and thus his ideas were accessible to only a select few. To this day the name Goethe implies privilege. After all, in Germany, as in most European societies, the educated class was a small elite. As time progressed, Goethe's most enlightened ideals became increasingly subverted. Finally, Goethe's name, having been appropriated by Nazi propaganda, lived on in the Goethe Eiche in Buchenwald.

What about the Goethe *renouveau* in the postwar era? Goethe served as a safe topic for many literary scholars who preferred not to write about more recent matters, former Nazis and Nazi *Mitläufer*, as well as Jewish exiles and survivors. For the majority of speakers of German, Goethe remained as inaccessible and irrelevant as he had always been. In postwar Germany the gap between highly educated and privileged individuals and groups and persons lacking access of the most elemental kind remained, and it continues to widen. This is a major problem and a challenge: can the disenfranchised of the diverse members of the European Union participate in European, including

German, literary culture and thereby experience the sense of connectedness that has always been the privilege of the cultural jet set of any given era while leaving the masses virtually unaffected? And if so, how? Or will such a sense of inclusion more likely be the product of commercial globalization and media culture?

At present, the only pervasive common culture affecting Europe and worldwide is one of genocide, ethnic cleansing, ex- and repatriation, exploitation, and economic and ecological disasters, a culture that defies well-intentioned interventions and other efforts on behalf of the victims. The universal language is the language of brutality, daily underscored and expanded by media images. Those who shape the literary culture of the future will have to be increasingly mindful of these realities, in particular of the victims' perspective and experience. As some of the best-informed and finest authors in the German language, including Edgar Hilsenrath, George Tabori, Doron Rabinovici, Torkan, Jeanette Lander, and Elfriede Jelinek have already begun to, it is incumbent upon German culture to embrace a compassionate global perspective rather than perpetuating rarefied, if only symbolic, court cultures for the elite.

NOTES

1. *Spiegel Online*, 15 May 1999, 17 June 1999.

2. Walter Benjamin, "Über den Begriff der Geschichte," in *Gesammelte Schriften*, ed. Rolf Tiedemann and Hermann Schwepphäuser (Frankfurt am Main: Suhrkamp, 1974), 696.

3. See, for example, Broder's retrospective on the former prime minister of Baden-Würtemberg, Hans Filbinger in Henryk M. Broder, "'Knechte des Gesetzes.' Wie der Rechtsstaat seine Richter fand," *Spiegel Online*, 17 May 1999.

4. "Neuer Stasi-Verdacht gegen Manfred Stolpe," *Spiegel Online*, 12 June 1999; Johannes Saltzwedel, "Bei Kaffee und Gebäck. Der legendäre DDR-Romanist Werner Krauss, NS-Widerständler und Kollege Victor Klemperers, war kurze Zeit Informant der Stasi—allerdings ein unbequemer," *Spiegel Online*, 7 June 1999.

5. "Milliardenklage gegen Dresdner Bank," *Spiegel Online*, 14 May 1999.

6. "Eklat um die toten Deutschen," *Spiegel Online*, 10 May 1999.

7. David Hudson, "Unsettling Accounts," *Spiegel Online*, 7 May 1999.

8. Gerhard Charles Rump, "Hinter den Kränzen ganz unverblümt. Die Ausstellung 'Zwischen Ideal und Wirklichkeit' zeigt Kunst von Frauen zur Goethezeit," *Die Welt Online*, Feuilleton, 15 May 1999.

9. Sibylle Fritsch, "Aus dem Vorhof zum Himmel. Der 85jährige George Tabori verabschiedet sich mit 'Purgatorium' von Wien," *Die Welt Online*, 31 May 1999; Michael Verhoeven, "'Ich bin ein Guru.' Und er ist ein Schüler. Michael Verhoeven porträtiert George Tabori," *Die Welt Online*, 15 May 1999.

10. Günter Franzen, "Der unendliche Binjamin und seine Fortschreibung," *Die Welt Online*, 14 June 1999.

11. Hans-Peter Schwarz, "Nie war sie so wertvoll wie heute," *Die Welt Online*, 15 May 1999.

12. Goethe Bytes, "Die Goethe Bytes sind ein Projekt der Online-Redaktion der Deutschen Welle," available online at www.goethe-bytes.de/.

13. W. Daniel Wilson, *Unterirdische Gänge: Goethe, Freimanerei, und Politik* (Göttingen: Wallstein, 1999).

14. Fanny Lewald, *Meine Lebensgeschichte*, 2 vols. (Frankfurt am Main: Helmer, 1988), 297.

DOES THE NEW NATIONAL GERMAN CINEMA HAVE AN AUDIENCE?

BETWEEN NATIONAL TELEVISION AND INTERNATIONAL OBLIVION: GERMAN CINEMA IN THE 1990S

Monika Treut

I am often described as a pleasure seeker, putting pleasure in the center of my films. I suppose this is true, and it is probably just a survival technique, since, as a nonmainstream German filmmaker, I not only write and direct my films but have also been forced to produce them. In reality the latter counts for three-quarters of the work: always hustling for funds. In filmmaking, writing and directing are the luxury, and producing and distributing the hard labor, the less fun side, the necessary suffering. I have also been described as having a strong penchant for sadomasochism; whether that's right or wrong, I beg your forgiveness for putting you in touch with the decidedly masochistic side of filmmaking—the financing and the film politics—in order to better understand the condition of German film in the 1990s.

What follows is a very compressed version of a highly complicated subject matter and represents only the personal viewpoint of this German woman filmmaker who often works abroad, whose work is seen and appreciated at international film festivals worldwide, whose films are distributed by small companies in the United States and Canada as well as in the United Kingdom, Germany, Holland, Australia, and New Zealand. Thus, I have both the perspective of the insider, who struggles with the German funding system, and the view

117

of the outsider: the female, postfeminist, queer, low/no-budget international filmmaker, who spends at least as much time abroad (i.e., outside of Germany) as "at home."

In most Western countries, foremost in the countries of the
European Union, in Australia, New Zealand, and Canada, the national
film industries are funded by the governments. There are two reasons
for this dynamic: (1) to fight the dominance of American productions
on their movie screens and TV stations, and (2) to protect their national
culture by funding the production of national films, often trying to
bundle funds through coproduction among several countries, mostly
excluding the United States, with exceptions in the English-speaking
countries. The Hollywood product has taken over the world and has
become synonymous with cinema—at least in the past thirty years.
However, film can be both mass entertainment and art. By nature film
is a hermaphrodite. Cinema has its roots in lower-class entertainment,
circus, vaudeville, variety. From its very beginnings, film has been an
art form as well as popular culture and sometimes both at once.

Seen through my eyes, the situation of the German cinema in the
1990s is miserable when compared with more productive decades of
the history of German film. From its very beginnings, film as the most
expensive form of culture/entertainment, had to be international, i.e.,
it had to be internationally distributed, in order to recoup the monetary investments. But before I discuss the present state of German cinema, I would like to undertake a brief survey of German film history
in the twentieth century.

From Weimar to the New German Cinema

In the late 1910s and 1920s, the premiere of one German film in
London was worth more than the premieres of twenty American films;
it was a major cultural event. Back then, the audiences and film professionals were looking at German films for technical invention, for
creativity and inspiration. Indeed, German film combined elements
from other art forms—architecture, theater, painting—and at times

these inventions were born due to the lack of funds. The premier example is *The Cabinet of Dr. Caligari* (1919), for which architects created light and shadows by painting directly on set decorations, thus transforming the influx of expressionist theater and paintings onto the film set. The early heyday of German cinema—*Nosferatu* (1922), *Metropolis* (1925), *The Blue Angel* (1929)—came to be known and admired around the world.

In the 1930s and early 1940s, the Nazis were highly aware of the power of cinema as mass entertainment and instrument of propaganda. In no other period in the hundred-year history of cinema has German film been granted more appreciation, money, and importance by its government. Contemporary German film politics still sub- or unconsciously holds a grudge against the medium that at one point in history had been made such a powerful voice of the politics of disaster.

In the late 1940s, the clumsy construction of a new culture in the Federal Republic of Germany had its greatest problems in the area of film—and those problems have continued until this very day. Both the Nazi propaganda films and the medium itself were viewed with fear and horror. Thus, beginning in the late 1940s and continuing through the present, German cinemas became the repository, the number one export tool, for the American film industry. Likewise, a huge number of artists—actors, writers, directors, cinematographers, editors—whose expertise in all fields of filmmaking had made German film an export item in the 1920s and 1930s, had been either killed or were forced to emigrate to America and thus make their living in the Hollywood film industry.

Even at its best and with very few exceptions, film in postwar Germany, in the late 1940s, the 1950s, and the early 1960s, was flat entertainment. No inventiveness, no inspiration characterized German film during this bland period. No international recognition was the result. The artsy and innovative part of the hermaphrodite film laid buried until the arrival of the so-called New German Cinema in the 1960s. The generation of Germans who were born during and after the war grew up with American popular culture. Indeed, except for the so-called *Heimatfilm*, there was no such thing as German pop culture.[1]

The second productive period of German cinema started in the mid-1960s and lasted until 1983, shortly after Rainer Werner Fassbinder's premature death. In addition to Fassbinder, among the leading directors were Alexander Kluge, Volker Schlöndorff, Margarete von Trotta, Werner Herzog, Wim Wenders (about whom a friend, a film critic in Los Angeles, recently remarked: "Wim Wenders? He's post-German, or beyond German").

Films of this period, such as Alexander Kluge's *Yesterday Girl* (1966), Fassbinder's *The Marriage of Maria Braun* (1979), Herzog's *Aguirre, the Wrath of God* (1972), still do have fans around the world, people who love them, collect them, talk and write about them, but, strangely enough, the films of this period are often better remembered in film and German departments of U.S. colleges and universities than in Germany.

The New German Cinema was a cinema of small budgets, with films often shot on 16mm film, frequently in black and white, and more often than not aimed at intellectual pleasure rather than at immediate gratification. These films are remembered for their original, daring, purist, controversial, and sometimes disturbing portrayal of this country named Germany. Please don't get me wrong: I am not nostalgic, I am not asking for this period to return—Germany has changed substantially. The New German Cinema, rooted in the 1960s and 1970s, cannot be brought back—not only Germany, but the world of global entertainment has changed tremendously.

Although the films of the New German Cinema were internationally acclaimed and shown at prestigious festivals like Cannes, Berlin, Venice, Montreal, and won international awards, they and their directors were not loved in their home country. This is especially the case with Fassbinder, who is, in my opinion, the most important of this group. I suppose this has to do with the fact that German film abroad or in Europe has always had the air of representing Germany, to be taken and perceived as more than film. To be sure, German officials were quite appalled at having someone like Fassbinder, openly homo-

and bisexual, someone who did not look and behave like the model German artist, represent Germany or German film throughout the world.

The Film Funding Law

At the core of the dilemma is the German film funding system created shortly after the Oberhausen Manifesto in 1963: film should be at once submissive to the rules of mass entertainment product and also be art and enlightenment for so-called educated minorities. Reacting to the hermaphroditic nature of film as art and product, a two-fold film funding system was inaugurated for (1) the culturally valuable film, which got its home at the Ministry of the Interior (quite interesting, as this is the home for film as well as for police and state security), and (2) the so-called commercial film fund.

This latter was and still is under the wing of the Ministry of Economics. Since Germany is a Federal Republic with no official ministry of culture,[2] the regional governments, in the early 1980s, started to furnish their own smaller film funding subsidy agencies separated into funds for commercially or culturally valuable films. From their beginnings to the present day these two systems were in competition.

In 1983 the German film funding law was changed: priority was given to "commercial films," although the international success of the New German Cinema was evident—*Time* magazine had just declared Fassbinder's *Berlin Alexanderplatz* movie of the year, and German films were widely popular at international festivals, international art houses, and on university campuses. What was missing was the booming box office. As industry export items German feature films could be compared to BMWs. The powers in Germany were and still are transfixed by national box office numbers. German films experienced bad times within Germany itself—the phrase became something like a curse: German film.

Creating a jungle of more rules was the outcome of the change in the film funding law. What resulted was (1) more awards for nationally successful films, and (2) the gradual killing of grants for films that performed poorly in Germany whether or not they had successfully crossed international borders.

Another result of the changing of the film funding law was that the number of film bureaucrats exploded. Every funding system was equipped with enough people to furnish the crew of a low-budget film production. Countless commissions were founded and peopled with the very same film bureaucrats, members of the political parties, the churches, etc.

Thus, in the 1980s, a new type of film producer was created—no longer was it favorable for filmmakers themselves to ask for funds; they were urged to have a producer to represent them. Film producers who were and are able to access money through the labyrinth of rules and regulations were not necessarily the ones who liked to take risks for their love of a particular project. They were not the ones who were inventive and open to new ideas. On the contrary, they were just as bureaucratic as the film funders.

One more reason for the downfall of risk-taking, inventive German films was a new development in the television landscape. In the 1960s and 1970s, German television, led by the two main public networks (ARD and ZDF) had been more or less supportive of the New German Cinema, and many of the creative films of the period had been coproduced with either the ZDF or ARD. In the 1980s, these channels grew more conservative. In the mid-1980s, commercially funded private television channels started airing their programs, aiming at immediate gratification and low entertainment. Daily soaps and cheap talk shows on all channels, including the public channels, filled in for documentaries, experimental works, and a variety of minority programming, pushing "the other cinema" to time slots after midnight, if such films were aired at all.

At the same juncture, the big screen likewise saw troubled times. Multiplexes started extinguishing art houses by offering more screens to the most popular productions. This phenomenon has become international in scope: multiplexes worldwide have more screens but tend to show less variety, i.e., the same blockbusters made in Hollywood. Audiences are no longer able to select what they want to see; they can choose between *Armageddon* and *Armageddon*.

No Allies for "the Other Cinema"?

There are hardly any allies to be found for struggling, risk-taking film-makers and the few producers who hope to produce quality films. The German print media do not offer a single film magazine worth reading. The small film magazine *Filmkritik* lasted only a few years. *Revolver*, another interesting but even smaller recent magazine, is poorly distributed and read by very few film aficionados.

In contrast, England has *Sight and Sound*, the excellent film magazine published by the British Film Institute, which devotes itself to a high standard of intellectual and entertaining journalism on current releases and film history. France offers the legendary *Cahiers du Cinema*, founded by Henri Langlois and supported by the French Cinematheque, where filmmakers like Godard and Truffaut began their careers by writing film reviews.

In Germany we mainly have glossy magazines that are basically part of the PR arm of the big distributors. They do little more than replace Hollywood publicity fodder. Hardly any independent thinking about film is to be found. Similarly, in daily newspapers the space for film reviews gets smaller and smaller every year.

The Success of "The New National German Cinema"

In the 1990s, after German reunification and with the German preoccupation with economics, the situation of the German film grew worse. The remaining cultural film funds were closed or stripped of their capital. Forces united to create commercial German films. The lack of enthusiasm, knowledge, and passion for film was glossed over by silly efforts to imitate Hollywood cinema on comparatively tiny budgets. From Los Angeles, American script doctors were flown in for countless seminars to teach German writers, directors, and producers how to create the perfect three-act storyline. This compensating for lack of ideas and courage, looking for inspiration through formulaic filmmaking, underscored the major concern: how to create larger market segments for German films in Germany itself. It is as if the New German Cinema had never existed.

Since the mid-1990s, we have the reverse situation: German film critics, film funders, and film politicians are finally proud of their films. 1997 was the most successful year for German film at the national box office since the 1950s. German films took 17 percent of the national box office. This amount may sound insignificant. However, this is quite respectable, as American films take about 85 percent at the box office each year, leaving about 15 percent for everything else. In 1997 films like *Rossini*, *Männerpension*, and *Werner, das muß kesseln* each sold more than three million tickets in Germany. Needless to say, these titles did not even make it to Holland.

Most of the nationally successful German films of the 1990s were comedies, and if they had not been screened in the cinemas, one would think they had been made for television. There is hardly any inventiveness to them. I call them biodegradable soap operas. Many of them are directed by television directors and the casts are peopled with German television stars. These films create worlds without any trace of social reality, the characters are cartoonish and flat, the relationship between the genders is modeled after official German gender politics in the 1950s. Nevertheless, these pretentious soap operas made for the screen, financed through government and regional funds, are supported by similar flat, glossy magazine journalism, creating a saccharine, provincial, and feel-good climate for Germans only.

Let us recall that in 1970, at the height of the New German Cinema, ten German films were invited to screen in Cannes, then and now the most important international film festival for world cinema, for art films as well as commercial films.[3] Strangely enough, in 1997, the year of the triumph of what I call the New National German Cinema, not a single German film had been invited to screen in Cannes. In this most successful year in decades, the film bureaucrats were ready to party in Cannes, but had no film to throw a party for. They spent the taxpayers' money anyway and ended up celebrating themselves. The icing on the cake was missing, however: international critical attention and the export of the nationally successful product simply weren't there.

After realizing that German comedies were hardly export items, the German film industry—although I hesitate to use the term since it is more a television industry—is hoping to export another genre that became nationally popular in the 1990s, narratives dealing with the German Nazi past: *Schtonk*, *Comedian Harmonists*, *Stalingrad*, and most recently *Aimee and Jaguar*. Some of these films are based on true stories, which could have been turned into internationally appreciated films, but most of these films, made by television directors, who also wrote the scripts, shy away from the complexity of the material and thus diminish the potential in the international marketplace.

At the end of my discussion of the miserable state of German film at the end of the millennium, I will further torture you with numbers. How much film money are we talking about? It is one of the best-guarded secrets of the "New Berlin Republic." It is much less than you think it is: the sum of the German official film funds is less than DM 200 million a year, just a bit more than $100 million, the equivalent of the budget of one big Hollywood studio action movie. We are indeed talking peanuts.

What strikes me is the cultural politics of this modern country named Germany. At the threshold of a new millennium, the majority of the money for culture in Germany goes to bourgeois art forms stemming from the sixteenth and the seventeenth centuries: the opera and the theater. My hometown, Hamburg, spends more than DM 260 million a year on the opera and on various city theaters, yet only about DM16 million on film, the art of the twentieth century, with half of it going to pure television productions. Cultural politics in Germany treats film as a second-class art form, still preferring outlived and live art forms such as the opera and bourgeois theater, still punishing film for valuing entertainment and kicking it out into the marketplace. The hermaphrodite called film is prostituted by German politicians, bad pimps made to walk the streets without protection.

If Goethe were alive today, would he be working in theater or film? The only thing I'm sure about is that Goethe, as the advocate of popular culture, would be working in the most contemporary art form, no matter how complicated and hermaphroditic it might be.

Is There Hope for German Film in Europe?

What about the European community? At the end of the millennium, the ultimate political energy of the European Union goes into economics. Film in the Euro political sense is now named "audio-visual material" in the context of the global economy and the dominance of the American product. Let me quote from an official brochure, *Audiovisual Policy of the European Union*:

> The demand of audio-visual material is growing rapidly. In this trade sector, in which the European industry still has a wide balance-of-trade deficit with the United States (6 billion dollars which means 25,000 jobs), priority needs to be given to making our companies more competitive in order to make the most of our cultural and linguistic diversity and to convert growth into jobs.[4]

I believe that the current Euro politicians are the morticians of European art cinema. I have to quote another voice, the voice of a French writer, Jean-Claude Carriere, who wrote or cowrote such remarkable films as Bunuel's *Journal d'une femme de chambre*, Louis Malle's *Viva Maria*, Goddard's *Sauve qui peut la vie*, and Schlöndorff's *The Tin Drum*. In a recent interview about the strategy of Euro-cinema Carriere states:

> The real problem of European Cinema is to go back to the roots of European Cinema. Not to American Cinema. And foremost not to be in competition with American Cinema. . . . American

Cinema tries to conquer the world by forcing a certain filmic stereotype on the world which destroys consciously every other form of cinema. . . . We gotta fight against it. . . . The only way is to convince the government like we convinced the French government, that Cinema is not a product but an expression which must be protected as part of the voice of the people.[5]

The French are fortunate. They are proud of their national culture, be it literature or theater or film. Indeed, unlike Germany, they spend much more money on their own national cinema.

British cinema as well is in good health, partly because of the language. English is *the* film language in the Western world of cinema. I will not delve into the specifics of the Italian, Spanish, Scandinavian, Greek, or Portuguese cinema. I will merely hint that unified European film politics is a pure joke. We have little more than official statements carried out by film-oblivious politicians in Brussels. One more statement from Brussels, another official guideline, the kind that, favoring the impossible imitation of Hollywood cinema, kills creative juices in any European culture: "The European cinema industry can hold up its head once more. It seems to have re-found the favor of a general public that is demanding films which are distinguished by a certain simplification of contents and standardization of forms."[6]

Inspirations for the Future

We are at a time when even Hollywood moguls have lost their wits, since film is expanding and changing its nature once again in a totally dramatic way. Permit me to remind you of a recent scandalously successful, total outsider production, *The Blair Witch Project,* with production costs of some $30,000 and U.S. theatrical grosses in the first six weeks of more than $130 million. This film, made by newcomers, is dramatically changing the nature of the most advanced film production system in the world.

The magic and operative word here is digital technology. *The Blair Witch Project* was shot on consumer digital video equipment, blown up for exploitation in the cinemas on 35mm film by the distribution company. In addition, it was heavily advertised on the Internet. These are but two of the new media that are revolutionizing the now old-looking film medium. Advanced digital technology is, in fact, changing the whole scenario of possibilities in making movies. It is becoming so inexpensive that the entire Hollywood system seems to be totally dated, part of an older century, unable to sustain its power structures into the new millennium. Hollywood is in a panic. This new digital technology is a powerful weapon in the hands of independent filmmakers. It provides the freedom to realize ideas without wasting time waiting for the funding of ideas.

This makes us equals, whether we are African, Asian, European, Australian, or American filmmakers. For the price of a used car, we can buy our film equipment. No excuses. The Danish film group Dogma 95 has led the way. The freedom of cheap filmmaking. And who knows the scenarios of the next millennium: movie theaters with Dolby stereo sound? Big 35mm prints? Why not simply download the newest Moroccan feminist film or the newest Hong Kong queer comedy via the Internet? The entire world of producing/making/resenting/selling film, whether art or entertainment, or both, is changing faster than we exchange words. The latest Hollywood blockbuster for teens soon will be aired via satellite simultaneously into countless movie theaters in cities around the world. No heavy 35mm prints, no Federal Express or UPS shipping. In the meantime, the fast- and ever-changing members of the world's digital, film, and Internet communities will have figured out totally new ways to finance and market the as yet unknown film products of the future.

The future in Germany? At the present moment, there is only one genre of German film that I find at all inspiring: the documentary film. Typically, today's documentaries are made on miniscule budgets, and are poorly distributed and barely supported by German film politics, yet are successfully crossing international borders.[7]

And in the narrative department? Only on rare occasions is there an outstanding German narrative film to be found, such as *Lola and*

Bilidikid.[8] This film was written and directed by Kutlug Ataman, an American filmmaker of Turkish descent living in the United Kingdom. *Lola and Bilidikid* was produced by a German company with German film production and television funds, shot in Berlin with a German and Turkish-German cast. Ataman, its writer and director, does not speak German, and his view on Berlin's culture and subculture is that of the total outsider. Nevertheless, this film captures the Berlin of the new republic in a more imaginative way than the majority of German narrative films of this decade could even dream to achieve.

NOTES

1. See Gerd Gemuenden's interesting study of German postwar culture, *Framed Visions* (Ann Arbor: University of Michigan Press, 1998).

2. The Social Democratic and Green Party government coalition has declared the former general manager of Rowohlt Verlag, Michael Naumann, "Staatsminister für Kultur." A year after the election, given the lack of funds, power, and political administration of Mr. Naumann, this seems to be more an election ploy than a political move.

3. Among these films were Syberberg's *Sexbusiness Made in Passing*, Werner Herzog's *Auch Zwerge haben klein angefangen*, Werner Schroeter's *Eika Katappa*, and others.

4. *Audiovisual Policy of the European Union* (Brussels and Luxembourg, 1997), 4.

5. Jean-Claude Carriere, in *Revolver* 3 (1999).

6. *Audiovisual Policy*, 16.

7. *Nico Icon* (1995), *Blue Note* (1997), *Didn't Do It For Love* (1998), just to name a few.

8. *Lola and Bilidikid*, written and directed by Kutlug Ataman, (Germany: Zero Film, 1998), in Turkish and German, 92 minutes, color, 35mm.

THIS CINEMA THAT IS NOT ONE?
MONIKA TREUT AND A
DETERRITORIALIZED GERMAN CINEMA[1]

David Levin

In this brief essay, I won't be offering my prognosis for the future of
German cinema in the new Europe—something I'm neither inclined
nor qualified to do. Instead, I'd like to consider Monika Treut's own
work in light of the dual visions afforded by this event: a prospective
and retrospective account of where things stand. I do so in part because
these are interesting and unusual films. Given the predictable, somewhat adolescent savvy of much recent German filmmaking—which
seems to alternate between weak imitations and pompous dismissals of
Hollywood—Treut's films head off in unfamiliar directions. As such,
hers is a cinematic road less traveled—indeed, programmatically so.
And yet, in the process of exploring new and unfamiliar territory, her
films arguably land us in strangely familiar places—where the play of
gender intersects with historical overdetermination. It is this—all too
German—conundrum that I would like to consider here.

   Treut's films are often bound up with questions of gender (and
here the phrasing would seem especially felicitous), but they would
appear to internationalize, or perhaps denationalize those questions.
Just consider the itinerary of sexuality in her films. Dorothee Müller,
the protagonist of *Virgin Machine*, leaves Hamburg and heterosexuality
and ends up in the lesbian subculture of San Francisco, while *Didn't Do
It for Love*—a documentary filmed in English—recounts the life of Eva

Johanne Chegodaieva Sakonskaya, a Norwegian who becomes Eva Norvind, a pinup girl and movie star in Mexico, who in turn becomes Ava Taurel, a professional dominatrix in New York.[2] Indeed, Germany doesn't figure at all in *Didn't Do It for Love* and *Female Misbehavior* (the latter, a collection of short documentaries shot in the United States and featuring figures on the margins of sexual identity).[3] In *Virgin Machine* (and, to a lesser degree, in *My Father Is Coming*), Germany figures in its absence—bound to an anachronistic heterosexuality that is comically inflected as personally and sexually untenable.[4]

In the face of this diverse group of films, I wonder whether it makes sense to describe Monika Treut's work in terms of a deterritorialization of German cinema—an oeuvre that implicitly formulates a critique of the very conditions that would enable a national cinema. Let me pose the question from an opposite perspective, that is, from the perspective of a programmatic search for a coherent national narrative. In *Stranded Objects*, Eric Santner analyzes the aspirations of revisionist German national historiography in the late 1980s, considering such notorious figures as Ernst Nolte and Michael Stürmer. "A national historiography," he writes, "assumes the task of salvaging—or perhaps more accurately, simulating—sites of identity formation no longer available in a cultural space defined by the double 'post' of the post-Holocaust and the postmodern."[5] (Indeed, it seems possible to amend—and therewith complicate—the point by adding a third "post," namely, the post-*unification*.) What would this mean for a national cinema—and, for that matter, what I have been labeling a deterritorialized cinema? To what extent does a German national cinema necessarily share much the same task as that which Santner ascribes to a national historiography? And to what extent can we read Treut's work as resisting such a simulation?

These questions are not as willful as it may seem. For recent—and no longer so recent—statements by some of the big (male) guns of the New German Cinema have suggested that the project for German film ought to be a kind of New Parochialism, inflected here as an anti-American, or rather, anti-Hollywood particularism. (And, indeed, if statements by Martin Walser, Botho Strauss, and more recently, Peter

Sloterdijk are any indication, the same argument would appear to hold for German Culture writ large.) With Hollywood filling in—once again[6] —as a new, if eminently familiar, even predictable villain in what Wim Wenders and Hans-Jürgen Syberberg both perceive to be a scripted foreign-ification of the German visual imagination, one wonders whether Monika Treut's work can't be seen as enacting (as it stages) an important difference.[7]

As Wenders and Syberberg long for a cinema that embodies a reassuring figuration of the land as properly unified, we might consider Monika Treut's work not just as leaving the nation behind, but as rendering the conceptual stakes of that departure. (Thus, the Irigarayan allusion in my title: hers would appear to be a cinema that is not *one*.) But what would this mean? Let us begin by attempting to map this deterritorialization. On the most obvious level, it strikes me that in her films the energies (and the very project) of deterritorialization are located in the bodies of her subjects. Quite literally. One of the dramaturgical nodes in Treut's work is the unwillingness or inability on the part of her subjects to occupy a unitary, stable identity—in body (e.g., Ellen Steinberg/Annie Sprinkle and Max Wolf Valerio in *Female Misbehavior* and again in *Gendernauts*), in sexual orientation (e.g., Vicky in *My Father Is Coming* or Dorothee Müller in *Virgin Machine*), or in the world (e.g., the multiple incarnations of Eva/Ava in *Didn't Do It for Love*). In her characteristic mixing of genres and styles, Treut's films reproduce this unsettled quality on a formal level. Here, then, we find ourselves in the thick of a dramaturgy of deterritorialization: in place of any sort of abstract or concrete territorial fixity, Treut's cinema repeatedly offers up a sense of thematic transitoriness as well as formal imperfection. Put a bit less abstractly: her interest in queer identities and forms is almost always dialectical, in flux.

But how might we characterize the national implications of the project of deterritorialization? In the few remaining pages of this essay, I would like to frame this question in terms of the paradoxical role of pain in pleasure—in sex, but also in the cinema. For Treut's thematic interest in the potential pleasures in pain—perhaps the only fixed place in her cinema—suggests a characteristic determination to explore and move away from fixed categories while at the same time suggesting the resilience of the national in the project of deterritorialization.

In *Women and the New German Cinema*, Julia Knight suggests that "since the patriarchal order constructs women's sexuality as essentially 'passive,' filmmakers such as [Birgit] Hein and Monika Treut have argued that what patriarchy fundamentally represses in women is their aggression."[8] Knight then goes on to quote from an interview she herself conducted in 1988 in which Monika Treut says: "I was thinking about images of women, about what images are most suppressed or repressed, and it was the image of *the cruel woman*." It is a point that recurs in Monika Treut's work.[9] What, we might ask, is the place of pleasure in that image of the cruel woman, and where, if at all, does history figure in it? For one of the things that Monika Treut's work suggests is the centrality (or, given the suspicion that her work justifiably casts upon the primacy accorded to things properly centered, the *importance*) of pleasure as a diegetic grail for which her protagonists search endlessly—and usually with an impish sense of adventure and a sober sense of the problems, if not the futility, of that search. Thus, in her films we don't just repeatedly encounter renowned proselytizers from what, in Middle America at least, is known as the sexual underworld—Susie Bright as Susie Sexpert in *Virgin Machine*, Annie Sprinkle as herself in *My Father Is Coming* and *Female Misbehavior*—but those characters tend to launch into extended explanations of the practices that they preach. Here, pleasure is not merely a diegetic aspiration but also a kind of spectatorial gambit, such that her spectators are implicated in that pleasure, which is, often enough, inflected as specifically spectatorial. That is, Monika Treut repeatedly positions viewers in places that are in the process of being recodified as pleasurable—places that viewers aren't necessarily used to occupying. Thus, for example, while men in general (and Marvin Moss, self-proclaimed "King of Porn," in particular) are barred from the infamous Baybrick club that Dorothee Müller visits on ladies' night in *Virgin Machine*, the camera—and thus, we in the audience—join her inside.

Of course, the project of taking spectators to places where they may have never been before is a relatively familiar means of allegorizing the project of seeing differently. Thus, to cite but two examples from the New German Cinema, in Werner Herzog's *Kaspar Hauser* and Fassbinder's *Querrelle* unfamiliar perspectives are simultaneously diegetic and formal—dramatized on screen, and reenunciated, we might say, in the aesthetics of that dramatization. The cruelty at play in Treut's films (and indeed, it is often literally at play) is not Fassbinder's emotional cruelty—which is, as Fassbinder himself never tired of pointing out, itself symptomatic of a certain residue of fascism in post-war (West) Germany.[10] Rather, Treut repeatedly zeros in on particular sexual practices that would enact—and, more important, *explain and demystify*—a highly theatricalized cruelty. Thus, in a number of her films, including *Seduction: The Cruel Woman*, *Didn't Do It for Love*, *Female Misbehavior*, and *Virgin Machine*, viewers encounter various modes and scenes of s/m sex. There is a didacticism here, but it is certainly not the familiar proto-Brechtian feminist didacticism of, say, Helke Sander.[11] Treut gives a voice—quite literally—to unfamiliar sexual practices (e.g., bondage and transsexuality in *Female Misbehavior*, or s/m in *Didn't Do It for Love* and *Virgin Machine*). That is to say, in addition to—and sometimes in lieu of[12]—dramatizing those sexual practices, Treut's characters often offer detailed, impromptu explanations of their mechanics and logic. And those explanations alert us to an important point—not just a thematic node in Treut's cinema, but in her politics as well: in the course of her films, we are repeatedly informed that the trappings of cruelty are deployed in the service of reassurance, protection, and pleasure.[13] With one key exception. For it strikes me that this claim to the salutary because reassuring, protective, and pleasurable qualities of s/m praxis coincides with the geographical removal of her work from Germany.

The claim in *Seduction: the Cruel Woman*, arguably the most "German" of her films, may amount to the same thing, but it certainly doesn't employ the same terms. Unlike the later films, where the s/m scene is clearly demarcated and localized, the scene of s/m in *Seduction* is much more expansive, characterizing Wanda's interpersonal relations as well as the highly theatricalized scenes of sexual performance in the gallery. Here, s/m seems to be less a theatricalized—let alone, a demystified—instrument of reassurance and pleasure than a way of life, albeit within the (multiple, layered) confines of the diegetic world.[14] Thus, what in the later films will emerge as a deterritorialized—perhaps we should say a para-German—sexual politics of reassurance could be said to retain a particular national resonance in this film. As such, the preponderance of an uninflected (if indisputably theatricalized and fictionalized) cruelty echoes uneasily with the mobilization of cruelty in twentieth century German culture. Put too directly: I wonder about the place of history in general, and of German history in particular, in this particular vision of an alternative erotics and theatrics of cruelty.[15] Does the historical overdetermination of the theatricalization of violence in Germany overburden the depiction of s/m in this most German of her films? And what is the relationship between deterritorialization and the reemergence of s/m practices as reassuring?[16]

It would appear that the move away from Germany coincides with a move away from s/m narrative and toward a more playful, less freighted circulation of s/m didacticism. Put otherwise: as the films move into uncharted territory they engage unfamiliar questions (about s/m or about gender fixity, for example). But in the process they also move away from familiar questions—questions about German history and its imbrication with aesthetic production. Why is this? And to what extent—if any—do these familiar (historical, even territorial) questions dog Treut's more deterritorialized films—which involve an ironic reinflection of Germanness to the extent that they have anything to do with Germanness at all? Indeed, in (and as) the end, I wonder whether this is a question raised by the films or by their paranoid interpretation? But at the risk of that overdetermined (and entirely too fixed) hermeneutic identity, I wonder how it is that history, uninvited, nonetheless comes to loom in the background of a restless search for misunderstood pleasures and complicated identities in a cinema that repeatedly leaves Germany behind in fact, if not in theory.

NOTES

1. My thanks to Temby Caprio and Katie Trumpener for their helpful comments on earlier drafts of this response.

2. *Virgin Machine* [*Die Jungfrauenmaschine*] (Germany: Hyäne I/II and NDR, 1988). *Didn't Do It for Love* (Germany: Filmgalerie, 1997).

3. *Female Misbehavior* (Germany: Hyena Films, 1992).

4. Germany is arguably absent in *Seduction: The Cruel Woman*, which, although it shows traces of being shot in Hamburg, takes place largely in the interior, highly aestheticized recesses of an s/m "gallery." I will return to this question later in this essay. *Seduction: The Cruel Woman* [*Verführung: Die grausame Frau*], cowritten, -directed, and -produced with Elfi Mikesch (Germany: Hyäne I/II, 1985). *My Father Is Coming* (Germany: Hyäne I/II and NDR, 1991).

5. Eric Santner, *Stranded Objects: Mourning, Memory, and Film in Postwar Germany* (Ithaca, NY: Cornell University Press, 1990), 52.

6. For the early history of this critique, see Thomas Saunders, *Hollywood in Berlin: American Cinema and Weimar Germany* (Berkeley: University of California Press, 1994). For a by-now canonical account of the diegetic function of the United States in the New German Cinema, see Eric Rentschler, "How American Is It? The U.S. As Image and Imaginary in German Film," *Persistence of Vision* 2 (Fall 1985): 5–18.

7. For an overview and critical account of Wenders's and Syberberg's recent positions, see the epilogue to Gemünden, *Framed Visions*, 195–213. For an English translation of Wenders's statement see "Talking About Germany," in *The Cinema of Wim Wenders*, ed. Roger Cook and Gerd Gemünden (Detroit: Wayne State University Press, 1997), 51–59.

8. Julia Knight, *Women ans the New German Cinema* (London: Verso, 1992), 162.

9. Knight, *Women*, 162. Treut's dissertation bears the title of her 1985 film, codirected with Elfi Mikesch, *Die grausame Frau: Zum Frauenbild bei de Sade und Sacher-Masoch* (Basel/Frankfurt: Stroemfeld/Roter Stern, 1984). Until the publication of her dissertation in translation, English

language readers will have to make do with Treut's essay "Female Misbehavior" (yet again, a title of one of her films) in Laura Pietropaolo and Ada Testaferri, *Feminisms in the Cinema* (Bloomington: Indiana University Press, 1995), 106–21, which sets out some of her ideas on the politics of masochism and offers a compelling account of the masochistic dynamic of German *Minnesong*.

10. See, in this regard, Thomas Elsaesser, "Fassbinder, Reflections of Fascism and the European Cinema," in *Fassbinder's Germany: History, Identity, Subject* (Amsterdam: Amsterdam University Press, 1996), 129–47, as well as David Bathrick, "Inscribing History, Prohibiting and Producing Desire: Fassbinder's Lili Marleen," and Johannes von Moltke, "Camping in the Art Closet: The Politics of Camp and Nation in German Film," both in *New German Critique* 63 (Fall 1994), special issue on Rainer Werner Fassbinder, 35–53 (Bathrick) and 77–106 (von Moltke).

11. Gerd Gemünden makes a similar point in the course of his discussion of Treut's work. See Gemünden, "The Queer Utopia of Monika Treut," in his *Framed Visions* (Ann Arbor: University of Michigan Press, 1998), 177–94, here 190–91. An earlier version of this chapter, with a helpful overview of the function of America in Treut's films appeared in Scott Denham et al., *A User's Guide to German Cultural Studies* (Ann Arbor: University of Michigan Press, 1998), 333–53; see, in particular, 334–37.

12. See, in this regard, Julia Knight's "The Meaning of Treut," 42, where Knight points out that the storm(s) of controversy surrounding the s/m content of *Seduction: The Cruel Woman* contrasts with the film's refusal to show sadomasochistic activity.

13. See Knight, "The Meaning of Treut," 42–3, as well as Treut, "Female Misbehavior," 113.

14. The film is inspired by Leopold von Sacher-Masoch's *Venus in Furs*. For an overview of the film as well as some of the controversies that have surrounded it, see Knight, "The Meaning of Treut," 40–43.

15. We are given a hint of the defensiveness that this question must arouse in Treut's essay "Female Misbehavior," 112–13: "There is but one

boundary: the respect for the possibilities of those with whom sexual practice takes place. And this deep respect that is sustained by every sadomasochistic mise-en-scène and that makes them possible at all is anything but fascistic. It ironizes actual human power relationships, insofar as rights of admission are granted only to those sovereign subjects who may, when and if they please, play the role of the master/mistress or slave, in order to fulfill their sexual desires. In contrast to actual violence, sadomasochistic violence is anarchic and free, libertarian and unbounded."

16. For it strikes me (and here the phrasing is infelicitous) that there is something akin to a cinematic *Wiedergutmachung* at play here, an attempt to reclaim, in the name of an impish humanism, practices that have been rendered taboo by their appropriation in or, more precisely, in the name of the Third Reich.

WHAT ARE THE SITES OF MEMORY

AND MEMORIALIZATION TODAY

AND WHAT SHOULD THEY DO?

CONFRONTING MEMORY AND MUSEUMS

Tom L. Freudenheim

An American commemoration of Goethe should take account of how he saw us from his far-off Weimar perch:

> *Amerika, du hast es besser*
> *Als unser Kontinent, der alte,*
> *Hast keine verfallenen Schlösser*
> *Und keine Basalte.*
> *Dich stört nicht im Innern,*
> *Zu lebendiger Zeit,*
> *Unnützes Erinnern*
> *Und vergeblicher Streit.*

> America, you have it better
> Than our old continent.
> You have no ruined castles
> And no basalt from ancient times.
> Nothing disturbs your tranquility,
> In our times,
> Useless memory
> And pointless argument.

Even Goethe knew that America was imbued with a different kind of psychohistory. That's why I think it is probably incumbent on an American Jew, currently working in Berlin, to present his bona fides before presuming to discuss the so-called New Germany and its relationship to the meaning of memory.

I was born in a slightly older Germany and emigrated to the United States with my parents in 1938, at the age of nine months. I never knew my older sister, who was murdered at Auschwitz. In spite of that, and the additional murders of uncles, aunts, and cousins, I think it is fair to describe my family as one with fewer Holocaust losses than those suffered by so many European Jewish families. In that sense, we shared the fate of numerous other, somewhat more fortunate, German Jews. But unlike many of their fellow transplants, my parents didn't speak German at home: "I don't want my children to learn the language of murderers," my father often said. When, as I teenager, I therefore couldn't cite Goethe, Schiller, and Heine, my disappointed father assured me that theirs was not the language of murderers; rather, it was Goethe, Schiller, and Heine! So I diligently memorized the poem with which my father first pointed out my ignorance: "Wer nie sein Brot mit Tränen aß. . . ." Goethe seemed to express my anti-German father's sentiments better than any poet writing in English. If the Germans were capable of perpetrating history's greatest savagery, their consummate man of letters was also the one to cite when commenting on the human condition.

That conflicting sensibility has followed me tenaciously ever since. Even before my first trip to Germany, in 1963, I had published a brief article attempting to come to terms with the conflict.[1] I had already sensed, at age twenty-two, that I was going to have to live in a world of Germans my own age—people whose relationship to the past was likely to be as confused as my own. Those are the people among whom I am now living and working, and I can't figure out whether my long-ago concerns indicate prescience or naiveté. In his newest novel, Ward Just reminds us of the problem: "Thing about a foreign country, you never know what you don't know."[2] But after years of traveling to Germany, I still haven't figured out whether it's a foreign country.

I am enamored of Berlin, where many of my ancestors lie buried in the lush and romantic ambience of the Weissensee Cemetery, and where I pass my great-grandmother's and grandmother's house en route to work every day. But I also need the recurring reminder of my cousin, Alfred Döblin's, 1928 reference to Berlin as *die unsichtbare Stadt* (the invisible city).[3] And he wasn't even looking at today's endless array of construction cranes! Of course this is something of a setup: the ironic contrast to fellow-Berliner Walter Benjamin's graceful vision of a nineteenth-century Paris and 1920s Berlin, replete with appropriately-attired flaneurs, so different from Döblin's vision of a tough and ugly Berlin.[4] Tourists, Döblin says, may find themselves drawn to the picturesque, but the reality lies elsewhere. We are not meant to apply a romantic sensibility to this place. If today's unemployment problem is less severe than that of Döblin's fabled Berlin—indeed, all those construction projects suggest the impossibility of any unemployment at all—nevertheless, much disquiet lies under the surface of the place I currently call home, and which some refer to as the "new Germany."

I want to raise several connected issues that arise more from my ongoing experience than from an academic baseline. There are the general observations made by someone who has lived and worked in Germany for about a year, comments which must be understood as Berlin-based. This is followed by a brief sketch of some of the Jewish issues with which I have been confronted during this time. As a museum person, I must raise questions about the role of museums in a place so rich in history and memory (and in museums!), and the relationship of museums to issues of memory. Finally, I suggest some of the challenges facing a Jewish museum in this extraordinary and almost *Judenrein* environment, while adding my comments about the meaning of memory to the overabundance of ways in which others have interpreted the concept.

Especially in this postreunification era, with its illusion of pan-Europeanism, Germany is simultaneously a European country like any other, while permeated by a sense of its uniqueness. That singularity is not the kind that usually distinguishes nations from one another. Rather, it comes from a viral relationship to recent history that infects everything about the present, and thus presumably about the future as well. I don't know that we can really speak of a "new Germany," even if today's is not pre-1945 or even pre-1989 Germany. Superficial globalization is no less common in Germany than elsewhere, with the signs of international commercialization everywhere cited as examples, creating a visual and mercantile repetitiveness that has invaded even the Third World. If the models of Madison, or Worth, or Michigan Avenues, or Rodeo Drive, can be extended to Munich, Düsseldorf, and Berlin, they can also be seen in Paris, London, and Madrid. The financial woes of Levi Strauss reflect the success of a product that created a worldwide blue jeans market, rather than the allure that distinct forms of dress once had in differentiating one culture from another. Germany's participation in this new world order is unremarkable. So perhaps we should be pleased to see the melding of styles—*ersatz Tracht* ("national" costume) worn with demin—since both reflect nineteenth-century creations that take hold in cultures only marginally related to either. The repetitiveness of automobiles, appliances, and electronic devices, even frames of reference—all suggest that one Western country is now pretty much like every other. And if we think this is only a recent phenomenon, we need only be reminded that by the 1920s KaDeWe was already engaged in marketing strategies similar to those of Macy's.

Such an essentially superficial picture—the one seen by many of our visiting friends—doesn't begin to describe what makes Germany—the new *or* the old—unique. In a recent *Frankfurter Allgemeine Zeitung* article, Ulrich Raulff aptly describes the country as a "Republik der Historiker" (republic of historians)—going further to suggest that this mania with history functions as a sort of *basso continuo* across large areas of discourse.[5] If ever there were a Sisyphean image of hopelessly heaving weight upward, it is the German with his burden of history. Damned if you do; damned if you don't. The external pressures are immense, and not without reason. But so are the internal pressures. Virtually everyone I know is struggling with the past; it is the monopoly of neither Gentile nor Jew.[6] And for them—as for most of us!—

this struggle means coming to terms with an inherited past—one created by others. I am haunted by an alternative notion, albeit from another context: "Everything in memory achieved a truth that was only a brand of falsehood."[7]

After all, this is no longer the Germany I first visited in 1963, when (like so many) I looked around at older people and wondered what they were doing a mere twenty years earlier. I now work and socialize in a world of people generally younger than I am. These are people concerned about personal and national image and accountability, wondering how to make their way through a labyrinth of fact and myth that would have stumped even a Theseus. In spite of the volumes devoted to the subject, I don't recognize *denial* as the worrisome issue. The real dilemma is in knowing how to handle *acceptance* of responsibility and living with such an unimaginably grotesque national past. I have heard German teenagers report that they are greeted with "Heil Hitler!" as they enter American high schools on exchange programs. Is this what we mean to encourage when we speak of the importance of memory?

An odd reflection of this is surely what seems like an abnormally large percentage of Germans enthusing about their visits to Israel. One sometimes has the feeling that a visit to Israel somehow constitutes an act of atonement, that it simply isn't another variation on the understandable German southward tropism and craving to find a place in the sun. Why would contact with Israelis and their land function as making amends? It certainly cannot replace the ongoing relationship with Jews that existed in pre-Nazi Germany (whatever way our nostalgia wants to define it), a relationship that barely exists now. Let's not forget that most Germans gradually turned on their Jewish friends and neighbors after 1933. Now there are too few Jews to constitute a very noticeable presence, so anti-Semitism is more of an abstraction: there aren't enough Jews to hate. Is it easier to see this exotic folk as people living in some faraway land? Do Jews in that way take on the same role as other Mediterranean people from countries one visits on idyllic vacations? I don't denigrate these attempts at figuring out how to handle the past and one's relationship to it. Quite the contrary! The complex interaction with Israel—not the *Wiedergutmachung* (reparations) issue, but the Israel vacation tour and study programs—constitute examples of the problematic and well-meaning efforts at figuring out the relationships with the Jewish pasts and present that permeate the environment in which I now live. The cypress-laden hills of Jerusalem notwithstanding, Israel as "der Toscana" is a questionable notion, at best. Tonio Kröger's ironic comments on Italy, "velvet blue sky, hot wine, and sweet sensuality," make for a bad fit when applied to the Holy Land. Goethe is also instructive here, when (writing about Naples) he contrasts his "German temperament and . . . determination to study and practise" with "easy, happy living" and looking at "the sea below, Capri opposite . . . probably nothing comparable could be found in the whole of Europe. . . ."[8] (Capri isn't in Europe?) Are we seeing a confusion between traditional German southward tropisms and the intensity of interest in Israel?

This new mania about Jewish everything may simply be an ironic reverse version of that classic Jewish syndrome—worrying what the goyim (non-Jews) will think: Germans are incessantly puzzling over how others see them. It is not mere paranoia, but a realistic response to legitimate outside pressures, forced on Germany ever since 1945, and subject to relatively little nuance or adjustment. All this sensibility and sensitivity to what "others" might think raises interesting questions. First of all, who *are* those "others?" I believe that this means Jews worldwide, but especially American Jews, and the American Jewish press. The illusion that these parties speak in unison won't bear up under careful scrutiny, but there is little doubt that a mistrusting and generally Germanophobic tone pervades a significant part of the American media. So the Germans must live always with that fear of: "See! The Germans haven't changed, after all."

Another fascinating related phenomenon is the number of young Germans studying what is generally called *Judaistik*—the equivalent of American "Jewish studies" programs—in universities. There are interesting comparisons here, which probably warrant some serious demographic research. In the United States a couple of generations ago, complex and in-depth Jewish studies could be pursued only at one or another rabbinical seminary and perhaps at Brandeis, proud of its position as the first Jewish-sponsored secular university. Columbia, Harvard, and a couple of other major schools had distinguished professors and a few related courses, but no general program as such was available—and indeed, there probably was no demand for it. (Hebrew was generally taught in a divinity school.) Today most major and many smaller American institutions of higher learning have Jewish studies programs, and a large number of advanced degrees are annually awarded in the field. Jewish students consitute the vast majority of participants in these programs.

By contrast, the same time span has seen the development of fewer, but somewhat equivalent, programs in German universities. There the preponderance of students are not Jewish. How could they be? There simply aren't very many Jews in Germany. Yet an amazing number of people applying for jobs at our museum have excellent Hebrew language skills, in-depth knowledge of (not just modern) Jewish history, often are even well-versed in the Bible and rabbinics, and have traveled and studied in Israel. I have met with a many of these people, interviewing them for jobs, and I work with some of them. They are impressive, indeed! We might see this as a natural continuation of the nineteenth-century *Wissenschaft* movement that was so crucial for the development of Jewish scholarship as we now know it, and which has German roots. I think that begs the question. This attempt to connect somehow—to find a way to understand what Jews were and are—is an essential part of the intellectual culture of today's Germany. And for those who don't manage it academically, there are films and television programs, lectures and books, and an endless array of newspaper and magazine articles that take up Jewish themes of one kind or another. This is not to suggest that some significant majority of Germans participate in this *Judaistik* studies trend, but it does reflect an important movement among the intellectual community.

I don't describe this to belittle it, but rather to cite these as signs representing the serious struggle that I see all around me. It is a struggle I respect! And that struggle is for me far more significant than awkward conversations I still have with older people, who remember or even participated in World War II in some way. Jane Kramer suggests that there are attempts conflating Germany and Germans with America and Americans—an approach she finds both dishonest and reprehensible.[9] Linking the Holocaust Nazi genocide with other kinds of serious crimes and violence is, indeed, reprehensible and has continued to be the subject of much debate. It has infused discussions about NATO or UN involvements in a number of so-called internal national struggles, and forms the background for War Crimes Tribunal discourse. But in Germany, these constant attempts at coming to terms with the past have an unnatural *earnestness* about them—unnatural until one remembers that many Germans generally approach many issues with a special kind of earnestness. "Jews" or "Judaism" as a subject of special national interest is problematic, especially where there are so few Jews. Recurrent underlying themes are always there in the form of "the Germans haven't changed!" or "have the Germans changed?" But what choice is there? A less earnest approach would be (and frequently is) subjected to even more severe criticism, suggesting Holocaust denial or historical amnesia.[10] On the other hand, I have not found myself engaging with German friends in what I would refer to as "generalization" discourse—equating Auschwitz with Hiroshima, or suggesting that ethnic cleansing in Kosovo is really comparable to the Holocaust.[11] Which is not to suggest that relations between and among disasters are not legitimate topics for discussion. But my (albeit limited) experience, socializing among and working with intellectually engaged Germans, gives little evidence of this as a topic with which most thoughtful people are currently concerned. And indeed genocide comparisons are generally acknowledged to be dangerous, almost taboo, territory in a place where Holocaust discourse is awkward, at best.

In the midst of this there is a special irony in what I see as the isolation of much of today's Jewish community in Germany—an isolation that seems at odds with so many parallel, but very separate, attempts to decipher Jews and their issues. Here I realize that my observations are very much that of an American Jew. While the term-of-use for com-

munity, *Gemeinde*, has official connotations,[12] it is even more problematic to speak of a Jewish community in Germany than it is in the States.
It's a fascinating, and for me, rather confused, picture. There are the
small number of Jews who lived in prewar Germany and either sur-
vived or returned: those self-proclaimed "German Jews." Their numbers were swelled by the Eastern European displaced persons or DPs
(many from what had been Poland)—that is, people who for one reason or other never left Europe when the DP camps were being emptied by resettlement in pre- and post-1948 Israel, the United States, or
elsewhere. That core of the Jewish community, German-speaking,
already second- and third-generation (it has, after all, been more than
a half-century since war's end) has had to live with personal, family, and
communal issues of great complexity. What were they doing there?
Why did they stay? How *could* they stay? These are questions I have
asked repeatedly, and the answers are as idiosyncratic as the people
being asked. Everyone has a different, often very emotional, sometimes
simply practical, story that explains his presence in Germany.

Is there an analogous situation here to the Germans themselves:
outsiders, primarily Jews, asking awkward and complicated, and even
embarassing, questions about one's relationship to history—about
one's ability to forget the past? If so, this might suggest the kind of
bonding between Jewish and non-Jewish Germans that external forces
often generate: united against a common enemy. Which would perhaps
mitigate against what I view as self-imposed social isolation of Jews
from their neighbors. While their histories differ radically, all of
them—Germans and Jews—have spent a half-century accused of a
perverse relationship with the past, and of not facing it honestly.

The last decade's subsequent additional influx of large numbers of
Jews from the former Soviet Union has added further complexity
(Americans would use the term *diversity*) to the Jewish population, as
has reunification, producing cultural conflicts among Jews often not
unlike those among the general citizenry. The idiosyncrasies of the
Jewish population component among Germans are then made all the
more acutely strange, from an American point of view, by the absence

of the kind of "hyphenation" that defines most of us. It's difficult to tell whether the old concept "German of Jewish belief" is still functional.[13] So if there is an ever-growing Jewish population in Germany, it looks to me as also ever more separate, somehow uncomfortable, always wary, yet also thriving. Quite a contrast to my father's Berlin recollections of growing up in what he called an "integrated" world in which he personally experienced anti-Semitism only after the onset of the Nazi period, in spite of the fact that he had become an ardent Zionist by the 1920s. I remain struck by the comments from Jewish friends that most Germans don't know enough about Jews. My reply, "So invite them to dinner!" is unanticipated in a social structure where separations between groups are often seen as unbridgeable. But one can always hope that generational transformations will alter the psychodynamics in this situation, although this would require serious shifts in the sociological plate tectonics, even beyond the German-Jewish world.

While I fail to see an American-type integration/assimilation among Jews in Germany taking place just yet, there are shared experiences and values here—concerns that mirror those of American Jews. As in many of our communities, a high intermarriage rate produces worries about whether one's grandchildren will be Jewish. At the same time, the Berlin Jewish community produces an intense level of cultural and educational activity that belies the ambivalence about living in isolation. But those activities are presented to primarily non-Jewish audiences—to full houses that would be the envy of most American Jewish presenters. With too few Jews for anything like neighborhood ghettoization, loyalty to a local or national Jewish community is mixed with a sense that Israel has special symbolic significance—even if relatives (and often progeny) have moved to the States. It is unlikely that the German-Jewish relationship to Israel has much in common with the German-non-Jewish tropisms. Understanding any of this is not easy—to the outsider the Jewish world in Germany is still a somewhat closed system, while insiders cynically observe its problems, assuring an American that there's no way to figure out the cosmos of what now constitutes German Jewry.

In the midst of such anomalies, what is the role of a Jewish museum? I would ask first, What is the role of any museum that deals with history? The truth is, we know too little about that. Do we actually have a clear sense of the sources from which most people learn about the past?[14] My guess is that such knowledge was once primarily transmitted through family and school, secondarily from books and museums. But is that still true in an age of sophisticated media—films, television, and the Internet? Clearly we still believe in museums—otherwise why would we keep building bigger and better ones? But while somehow instinctively trusting in the honesty of public institutions, we are also more attuned to the ways in which information is manipulated. We no longer speak of *history*, but rather of *whose history*. And that means we also differentiate between *memory* and *whose memory*.

A fascinating case in point is the recently opened megaexhibition organized by the Deutsches Historisches Museum (German Historical Museum) in Berlin's Martin-Gropius-Bau. Commemorating both the half-century of the Federal Republic and a decade since German reunification, the exhibition "draws a provisional balance of contemporary history, stimulating and self-critical at the same time. . . . Views are shaped by recent events and by personal experience."[15] There are several key terms here. "Provisional" suggests that the museum wants to clarify its stance regarding any opinions expressed—they may or may not bear up under academic examination or withstand the test of time. This is perfectly reasonable, but we are not accustomed to such candor from a museum. "Balance" immediately implies the possibility of its opposite—that is, imbalance. But who determines balance, and is there really consensus about such things? "Self-critical" assures the museum visitor that the museum is not going to whitewash whatever parts of the past might lend themselves to such an approach—an especially difficult problem in Germany, where it appears impossible comfortably to view the past. "Personal experience" is, in some ways, the most comforting to me—because I want to know that the museum's historians are expressing views shaped by their own experiences, rather than suggesting some distanced pseudoscientific point of view.

This remarkable exhibition is both invigorating and disturbing, trying as it does to satisfy a range of needs. These historic five decades
must be made manifest. But doing so involves describing an ugly end
to an ugly war, an occupation, reconstruction, and forty years of two
wholly different and competing governmental and social systems, as
well as the bitter end of one of those systems. The museum tries, with
some success, to validate the issues separating the two Germanies—
not uncritically, sometimes too evenhandedly, sometimes cynically. The
challenge is to make history meaningful to a range of visitors—presumably primarily Germans, but others as well. But insofar as the
GDR's past is concerned, can one simply invalidate four decades (a
couple of generations) of history—suggesting that an entire country
was amiss in all respects? The accomplishment of this current exhibition suggests problems yet to come, as the staff of the Deutsches
Historisches Museum confronts the years 1933–1945—which presumably they will do when their renovated and expanded quarters
open in a few years.[16] But how will issues such as "provisional" and "balance" play out then? And since there will be even fewer "witness, survivor, perpetrator" people alive at that time, will "personal experience"
even come into play?

This dilemma lies at the heart of all historical museums. It is not
just a German problem, as I found out when I was caught in the
middle of the notorious Enola Gay exhibition controversy at the
Smithsonian Institution a few years ago. "Survivors"—in this case sur-
viving crew members—recounted their versions of the bombing of
Hiroshima for video cameras. Quite understandably, those versions,
told by elderly men recalling something that took place fifty years earlier, were sometimes at variance with contemporaneous documents
and newspaper accounts.[17] "There are no versions of this story!"[18] we
were often told, as the controversy tore apart the Smithsonian and
became fodder for manipulative news accounts.[19] "Tell it the way it happened—that's all," we were instructed, so the bowdlerized version of
the exhibition finally presented pretended to lay out an uninterpreted
narrative, as if that were possible. The only permissible mediators of

the past were the heroic old men who had actually flown this historic mission—the "survivors" [sic] whose credibility was deemed to be impeccable. The institution's failure of nerve has had serious negative repercussions for museums in the States, where a new uncertainty has now been created in regard to the potential for interpreting historical controversies in a museum context.

A related problem can be seen in an extraordinary exhibition recently on view at Dresden's Hygiene Museum. Entitled "Der Neue Mensch: Obsessionen des 20. Jahrhunderts" ("The New Man: Obsessions of the 20th Century"), this project reflects wonderfully Pope's aphorism that "the proper study of mankind is man."[20] Working its way from nineteenth-century scientific and intellectual theories in physical anthropology, and its subagendas with implications about the perfectability of the human species, the exhibition moves through various fin-de-siècle health movements that are connected with, but not always specific to, Germany. Indeed, whether in Dalcroze and Isadora Duncan, in health food, nudism, or gymnastics, national boundaries were constantly crossed. How this sense of creating an ideal transnational human being was then incorporated into Nazi ideology recontextualizes that theory in a rather disconcerting manner. It is a context we don't want to see, especially when the exhibition propels us forward into our own age of genetic engineering, and its ethical implications. Implicit in the Dresden exhibition is our tendency to grasp for ways of disentangling the Nazi from other kinds of racism, and we are confounded by our inability to make this work for us properly.

I am reminded of Heinrich Heine's cynical verse:

> *Unbequemer neuer Glauben!*
> *Wenn sie uns den Herrgott rauben,*
> *Hat das Fluchen auch ein End—*
> *Himmel-Hergott-Sakrament!*

> Uncomfortable new belief!
> If they deprive us of the Lord God

the curse also has an end—

Heaven—the Lord God—Sacrament!

Inconvenient new beliefs, Heine suggests, deprive us of our sanctioned ability to curse. In our own day, these new and different ways of looking at the world threaten a half-century of traditional approaches to the past. Our comfort level is increasingly reduced as we work with and toward complexity.

It's not news that museums of national history tell the stories that they feel obliged to tell. But that obligation will shift with transformations in national self-perception. The suggestion of memory is implicit. Nations, like individuals, require memory. But whose memory? And can variant memories, or versions, be concurrently put forth? Can the history museum—somehow implicitly understood to be the purveyor of "truth"—actually suggest that there are such things as "truths?"[21] This is not a German problem alone, even if the world enjoys suggesting that it is. Indeed, an observer of this German struggle over the past, ritualized almost to the point of a tauromachia, is far more invigorating than it might be elsewhere—precisely because of the over-consuming self-awareness in this nation of historians. Other countries could learn something from these self-conscious forays into figuring out ways of presenting the past.

These challenges obviously confront our efforts to create a Jewish museum in Berlin. We know the general outlines of the story we plan to present—a focus on the history of Jews in Germany (or German lands, fairly broadly defined) from Roman times to the present. It is not a standard five-thousand-year overview of Jewish history and religion around the world.

That suggests we have simplified our task. Not so. What, for example, are the limits of what we will call "German-Jewish?" Modern Germany is quite different from its various earlier parts with their often-shifting borders. German language also makes for only a partial binding definitional tool, but in some instances it is a critical one. What role does Yiddish, one Jewish adaptation to German cultural hegemony, play in this story? Maintain a breadth to the museum's confines of interests, while not losing sight of the need for specificity to assist the visitor—these are challenges for all museums. We will need to figure out whether we speak of "German Jews" (an important term of use with interesting sociological implications) or "Jews in Germany." While our narrative is meant to encompass all of Germany (whatever that is), this question of "which Jews" we describe is especially important in Berlin—a city that always attracted a range of populations from elsewhere. One needs only to read Isaac Bashevis Singer who, after all, wrote in Yiddish, to realize the central role Berlin, and indeed Germany, plays in a Jewish history experienced by Jews from Poland for whom the city was a critical social, cultural, and intellectual vortex. Canetti and Celan, two linguistic German Jews, are others who make this point for us, since both are deeply embedded in what generally passes for German-Jewish culture.

One problem of "memory" lies in its potential for being the enemy, rather than the accomplice, of the historian. Perhaps memory should be reserved for art, distinguished from history. Apropos of a fictional character contemplating World War II, Ian McEwan writes:

> He was struck by the recently concluded war not as a historical, geopolitical fact but as a multiplicity, a near-infinity of private sorrows, as a boundless grief minutely subdivided without diminishment among individuals who covered the continent like dust, like spores whose separate identities would remain unknown, and whose totality showed more sadness than anyone could even begin to comprehend; a weight borne in silence by hundreds of thousands, millions. . . .[22]

And there remains always the question of remembering what one has never experienced. Indeed, this is a Jewish obligation. One version of the Decalogue commands, "Remember the Sabbath day to keep it holy" (*zachor et Yom ha-Shabbat le-kadsho*)[23]—presumably on the assumption of prior knowledge about the day and the need for its sanctity. The

Hebrew word for memory—*zicharon*—comes from that same "remember" word in the Ten Commandments, as does *yizkor*—meaning remembrance, and a Jewish term-of-use for a memorial service. Implicit in all of these concepts is the notion that one has somehow experienced what is being remembered. Lisa Lewenz, the creator of a superb recent film about her grandmother's Berlin of the 1920s and 1930s, *A Letter without Words*, has described to me the frightening experience of finding her way in Berlin—a strange city, on her first visit—as if she somehow had a memory of the place imprinted on her genetic code. Memory is a strange concept, indeed!

The Passover Seder liturgy requires that "in every generation, each person should feel as though he himself had gone forth from Egypt"[24] That individual reexperiencing of history is also implicit in the recitation of Christ's Passion during Easter Week, which is replete with suggestions of undergoing a kind of annual personal martyrdom. Such feelings underpin the mystical power of St. Theresa, and the stigmata of St. Francis, but they are not restricted to Christianity. Perhaps the concept of memory functions most persuasively using this self-insertion into the past as a model, by compressing *reexperience* with *memory*.

But how can we make this work in a history museum, especially in a Jewish museum that aims to address a wide range of audiences? One really cannot ask them all somehow to reexperience a past they never knew? Or, focusing more precisely on the ever-present issue in today's Germany, can we honestly suggest that memory is what we are after in relation to German-Jewish history and specifically the Holocaust?

I would suggest an alternative approach, which is in fact what most of us are really taking, even if we use varied and imprecise terminology to describe it. We really want people to "know" about the past, to "learn" about it. There is an assumption—untested, alas—that this knowledge has some therapeutic and prophylactic value: when known, the so-called mistakes of the past will presumably not be repeated. Teaching, conveying information, is a great deal more difficult than discussing memory. Zahava Doering, who has done seminal research in the field of museum communication, suggests that museums move from considering the visitor as a "guest" to addressing him as a "client."[25] This shift is important, because the "guest" approach is the familiar one: visitor education based on the premise that the museum experience will do good things to and for the visitor. The "client" approach is more challenging, coming as it does from a marketing framework that wants first to identify who the client is. Further, it suggests accountability to this client. Thus, in Doering's words, "the institution acknowledges that visitors, like clients, have needs, expectations and wants that the museum is *obligated* to understand and meet" [italics mine].[26]

For successful communication, museums will need to understand something about how both history and memory fit into the needs of their visitors. I am not suggesting that we obliterate the "memory" notion from our approach to the past. But I do believe that insistence on memory as a museum mission is a misapplied means of handling issues that require a more nuanced understanding. Yes, memory and memorialization have their utility. Most religious observance depends on the idea. And since memory is also often subject to serious misuse, one shouldn't count on its eternal benefits.[27] Virtually every current regional conflict around the world is generated by claims to memory. As a museum person, I feel less committed to concerns about memory than to grappling with the infinitely more problematic questions surrounding the learning process.

And that remains the most difficult problem, because we know so little about how people learn, especially in connection with non-classroom experiences, which are the most frequent. Nor do we really understand much about the role of museums in transmitting information about the past. That's not a very comforting thought for one engaged in what I do. At the risk of bold overstatement, I would suggest that in an art museum, where aesthetic concerns often have primacy, it may be useful, but not essential, that one fully understand the iconography, biography, or geography of what is being viewed. Thus the aesthetic dimension might be available even to the uninformed or unbeliever, although this is not to minimize the importance of "learning how to look." History museums lack that advantage, as was made especially evident while setting up the display of the Enola Gay in 1995. The overwhelming scale of the airplane and an explanation of its technological achievement for its time—both somehow corresponding to the aesthetic experience—didn't begin to suggest the power of the aircraft's meaning in history. And if there were lessons to be learned from Hiroshima, there was never consensus on what those lessons were. On the other hand, the exhibition created the illusion that memory was not only a key player in the contentious discourse, but should be given primacy over historical information. And in that sense memory became the rival, if not the enemy, of history.

So what is the role of a Jewish museum in Berlin as it relates to memory at this time in Germany's history? In an environment in which Jews remain exotic, both because of their victim status and their resultant numerical paucity, do we increase this sense of exoticism by placing Jews and their history in a museum—traditionally a voyeuristic environment? Will the curiosity about anything Jewish that permeates so much of German life be satisfied by a museum, or will that situation exponentially increase Jewish curio status? Non-Jewish Germans seem anxious to know more about Jews, while Jewish Germans want their countrymen to know more about them. This appears a propitious moment to concentrate specifically on addressing those needs, but a museum's role in this effort remains unclear.

This is a critical and transitional moment for Germany. Credit might be given to reunification or to the shift of the capital from Bonn to Berlin or to the phases of historical self-examination that have followed one after the other for five decades. I believe the source is elsewhere: that mysterious process known as "time." It is supposed to heal all wounds, but we know that isn't always so. Each of us is subject to time in a wide range of ways—physically and mentally. Even when we try to alter time's effects with potions and motions, we know we can have impact only at the bare edges.

That is where we now find ourselves with regard to memory and memorialization. That is why the Bubis-Walzer debates, while politically stimulating, must be seen more as generational steam-letting than as meaningful signposts to the future. That is why most of the questions involved in the interminable Holocaust Mahnmal (Memorial) discussions—bigger or smaller, designated site or elsewhere, assuring memory or confirming *Schlussstrich* (i.e., end of the debate)—are also ultimately irrelevant. Time takes care of the past receding, whether or not we want it to. And that receding past is already modulating views of the Nazi period and the Holocaust—whether we like it or not. There are always succeeding generations. Time takes care of that.

Two interesting recent examples, which have crossed over, to some degree, into pop-culture, demonstrate this shift. Both Bernard Schlink's novel *The Reader* and Roberto Benigni's film *Life is Beautiful* handle Holocaust stories in somewhat unconventional ways—reflecting the "uncomfortable new belief" about which Heine expresses such concern. The works shift the paradigms in ways that artworks have traditionally fed feelings of discomfort. While neither is a wholly satisfactory work of art, each confronts the past as part of its creative effort, but within different parameters from those set by what has become almost canonical in how to approach the Holocaust as grist for a creative mill. Schlink's somewhat distanced stance almost suggests a sense of moral neutrality, just as Benigni's bringing humor into a film about deportation and death can be irritating. Each is equally interesting for the discourse it has generated as for itself. It may be in these creative realms that we will see the most interesting new ways of handling questions of memory, and perhaps even its intersection with history.

All of this suggests that we are at the initial stage of a *new era* in respect to Germany's recent past (i.e., rather than a "new Germany"). This shift is exemplified in part by reactions we receive when we tell people that we plan to integrate the Holocaust into a larger panoramic narrative about German-Jewish history. Common reactions are: "Can it be integrated?" "Why should it be integrated?" "What do you mean: integrated?" Because, as they used to say, time marches on, these questions will answer themselves. And with that march comes the inevitable impact on memory, the transformation into its pale shadow, which we call memorialization.

We are fortunate to live in an age that provides better recording devices than those available to our ancestors. So photos and films, and letters and lists, and much more will remain available for study and research—less as memory jogs, than as historical documentation. The ever-growing number of survivor interviews can add personal depth and nuance to the documents—although into those personal accounts must also be factored the time lapse between direct experience and interview – yet another memory problem. Indeed, the expanded technological ability to provide so-called historical documentation (e.g., video and audio interviews) is likely to prove a better resource for studies of memory and the influence of ancillary information of memory than for actual historical study.

But all documentation (and museums, of course) are also subject to the effects of time. We are all *less* imprisoned in the past than we may think. I certainly hope that the Germans will gradually learn that as well. Goethe, the celebrant of this jubilee year, gave us a clue in the last line of that poem my father embarassed me into memorizing: ". . . alle Schuld rächt sich auf Erden" (all guilt avenges itself on this earth). Goethe understood that things even themselves out, even if we're not quite sure how. I see myself as living through this process, observing it with interest, fiddling around with it at the margins, but ultimately knowing that these things take care of themselves. It may not be a feeling of power, but it certainly is a feeling of comfort.[28]

NOTES

1. Tom L. Freudenheim, "Unser Kampf," in *variant* (Cincinnati, 1961).

2. Ward Just, *A Dangerous Friend* (Boston: Houghton Mifflin, 1999), 14.

3. Alfred Döblin, "Geleitwort," in Mario v. Bucovici, *Berlin* (Berlin: 1928).

4. Walter Benjamin, "Paris, Capital of the Nineteenth Century," in *Reflections*, trans. Edmund Jephcott (New York: 1978).

5. "Bigband Zeitgeschichte," in *Frankfurter Allgemeine Zeitung*, 21 May 1999, 49.

6. For a few recent discussions on this never-ending topic see Toby Axelrod, "A Vote for Memory?" *The Jewish Week*, 25 September 1998; Ian Buruma, "War Guilt," *The New York Times*, 29 December 1998; Moritz Schüller, "Hitlers Aufsteig in zwei Minuten," *Die Welt*, 30 March 1999; Jost Kaiser, "Der auserwählte Folk" *Süddeutsche Zeitung*, 26 May 1999; Heinz Berggruen and Michael Blumenthal, *Der Taggsspiegel*, 25 June 1999; Rafael Seligmann, "Der Musterjude," *Die Welt*, 27 August 1999; Moshe Zimmerman, "Ein deutscher Jude," *Süddeutsche Zeitung* 28/29, August 1999.

7. David Guterson, *East of the Mountains* (New York: Harcourt, Brace, 1999), 33.

8. J. W. Goethe, *Italian Journey*, trans. W. H. Auden and Elizabeth Mayer (San Francisco: North Point Press, 1982), 207.

9. Jane Kramer, *The Politics of Memory: Looking for Germany in the New Germany* (New York: Random House, 1996), xvi–xvii.

10. The recent Bubis-Walser debates were only the most recent manifestation of this earnestness. And in this case it wasn't simply the discourse among two men of the same Holocaust-experienced generation, but the intense level of general interest generated by their exchanges; this was a subject about which everyone was expected to have a serious opinion.

11. See, for example, Alan S. Rosenbaum, ed., *Is the Holocaust Unique? Perspectives on Comparative Genocide* (Boulder, CO: Westview Press, 1996); Peter Novick, *The Holocaust in American Life* (Boston: Houghton

Mifflin, 1999), 110–112; and Richard Cohen, "A Look into the Void, Kosovo as Holocaust Analogy," *The Washington Post*, 16 April 1999.

12. The *Gemeinde* (community) is an entity recognized by the government, which assists in collecting taxes from *Gemeinde* members. While somewhat differently organized from the Christian church system in the post–World War II era, it nevertheless reflects a special church-state relationship.

13. Ironically, this discussion emerged again recently in the many obituary notices and op-ed pieces written throughout Germany following the death of Ignatz Bubis on August 13, 1999.

14. The increasingly universal ignorance of history, not simply an American phenomenon, is obviously a related issue.

15. English text in exhibition brochure, "Einigkeit und Recht und Freiheit, Wege der Deutschen, 1949–1999," Deutsches Historisches Museum, 1999.

16. The DHM has, in fact, already grappled with the Nazi period in earlier, somewhat tentative, exhibitions. Now closed for major expansion and renovations, the museum presumably will address the full scope of twentieth-century German history when it reopens in 2001.

17. See Martin Harwit, *An Exhibit Denied: Lobbying the History of Enola Gay* (New York: Copernicus, 1996), especially 126–49. See also Edward T. Linenthal and Tom Englehardt, eds., *History Wars: The Enola Gay and Other Battles for the American Past* (New York: Metropolitan Books, 1996).

18. Linenthal uses a wonderful term for this: the "enduring truth of first interpretations."

19. See Harwit, especially 238–60.

20. Nicola Lepp, Martin Roth, and Klaus Vogel, eds., *Der Neue Mensch: Obsessionen des 20. Jahrhunderts* (Ostfildern-Ruit: Cantz, 1999).

21. Linenthal, citing Marita Sturken, has suggested that history is "a collective and mobile script."

22. Ian McEwan, *Black Dogs* (London: Vintage, 1998), 164–65.

23. Exodus 20:8.

24. *A Passover Haggadah*, ed. Herbert Bronstein (New York: Central

Conference of American Rabbis, 1975), 56.

25. Zahava Doering, "Strangers, Guests or Clients?" conference paper, Smithsonian Insitution, Institutional Studies Office, March 1999.

26. Doering, "Strangers, Guests or Clients?" 1.

27. Suggested by W. Michael Blumenthal.

28. In the process of working on this essay, I benefited from a number of interchanges with family and friends. I want especially to note with gratitude the many conversations with with my wife, Leslie, my sons, Sascha and Adam, my mother, Margot Freudenheim, and my cousin, Helga Döblin. I am grateful to Horst Olbrich for help with citations, to Eva Söderman for her comments, and to my son Adam for his editorial assistance.

THE TASK OF MUSEUMS

Howard A. Sulkin

I begin with a story. Many years ago, when my wife and I first moved to Chicago to attend this university, we cabbed one evening to the near north side to have dinner with friends. I said to the driver that we wanted to be taken to an address on Goethe Street. The cab driver exclaimed: "There ain't no such street! What did you say the name of the street was?" I repeated "Goethe" two or three more times to the driver's consternation. To ease the situation, I finally wrote out the address. The taxi driver read my note and yelled at me: "Why didn't you say so? Why didn't you just tell me that you wanted to go to Go-thee Street?"

This is not meant to be an attack on the cultural or linguistic education of Chicago taxi drivers. Instead, I tell you this story, perhaps, to suggest that I feel similar to them as I make this presentation. Both as a museum director and as a discussant, I think that I know where I want to go, but I need some help in getting there. Others want to help me get there, but they feel that I'm not cooperating. Finally, different people, with differing points of view, think that we're saying the same thing to one another, but neither is listening to the other.

Let's begin our discussion at the beginning. For Judaism, faith is memory—recall of the past is a call to faith in the present.[1] As the great Jewish philosopher, Abraham Joshua Heschel, said:

When we want to understand ourselves, to find out what is most precious in our lives, we search our memory. . . . That only is valuable in our experience which is worth remembering. Remembrance is the touchstone of all actions. Memory is a source of faith. To have faith is to remember. Jewish faith is a recollection of that which happened to [the people of] Israel in the past....Recollection is a holy act: we sanctify the present by remembering the past.[2]

In the approximately dozen Jewish museums that exist in Germany, and the more than seventy-five existing in Europe, this struggle for recollection and sanctification continues. But what is the purpose of Jewish museums in Europe? In Europe, unlike America, there are places of Jewish history—homes, synagogues, cemeteries, so is there the same need for Jewish museums? In some cases, because of the almost total absence of Jews, these museums appear as contemporary versions of Hitler's dream for a museum to a "destroyed race," the Jewish museum that he planned to build in Czechoslovakia. Are these museums willing to confront, as the new Paris museum does not, such hard issues as the realities of national participation in the Holocaust?

The European respect for history is significantly different from the antihistorical view of many Americans. Despite Goethe's dream of an international culture, learning from the past, learning from others, receives short shrift here. The pioneer spirit of the rugged American still predominates our psyches. Everything starts afresh when we rise in the morning, everything is new and unprecedented, what is important is the here and now. Everything will have a happy ending if we only work hard enough.

It is not clear whether German Jewish museums specifically, and European Jewish museums generally, are facing these same questions. It is reasonable to suggest that each American Jewish museum is a microcosm of the American Jewish community. The problems and issues confronting each Jewish museum reflect the problems and issues confronted by contemporary Jewry as a whole. These include fundamental concerns such as: Who is a Jew? What is Judaism? Jewish/non-Jewish relations, anti-Semitism, authenticity vs. relevance, content concerns vs. audience development concerns, the place of Israel in Diasporan existence, and Jewish survival and revival. The European museums must confront these same issues, but the priorities given to each of them, and the resultant interpretation, reflects the local reality, and to whatever extent, an international perspective.

Let me summarize for you the eight key problems facing Jewish museums in America, to a significant extent Jewish museums in Europe, and in fact, museums of all types everywhere. I contend that each of these has an impact on how museums deal with memory and memorialization.

1. **Lack of Clear Mission.** There is an absence in many Jewish museums of a clear conceptual framework and an action plan for its implementation. This has left these museums bereft of a structure for coherent programmatic design and implementation, as no museum can do everything, nor be all things to all people. This lack of conceptual clarity and coherence directly impacts upon the most pragmatic day-to-day concerns of collection policy, museum administration, and museum education. This lack undermines a museum's ability to program creatively for memorialization.

2. **Museum as a Term.** The term "museum" derives from the Greek, meaning "Temple of Muses." The words "muse" and "museum" clearly do not translate comfortably in either Hebrew or Yiddish. The muses are goddesses, and classical Hebrew has no term nor any understanding of such entities. Neither is the notion of a temple of muses compatible with Jewish thought. The term "Jewish museum" is, therefore, not only a linguistic misnomer, but a contradiction in terms. Jews never built a temple to Moses, much less to muses.[3] This classical definition of a museum focuses our attention on "showing off" the treasures in our treasure-house, instead of on more complex and taxing ideas such as memory and memorialization.

3. **Motivation.** Perhaps the reasons for why Jewish and general museums are being built today are so overwhelming that few can ever meet the expectations of their builders. Museums are supposed to fulfill their traditional roles of collecting, preserving, and educating, and at the same time, serve as centers of pride for ethnic, geographic, or religious groups, as means to assuage guilt and recognize contributions of the great and the not-so-great, as attractions for tourists, and as magnets for new industry and construction in cities facing decline.

4. **Building as Medium.** The focus for new museums is now on the architect and the building and not on the collections, exhibitions, or the educational programs. Examples of this abound on both continents: the Jewish museums of New York, Los Angeles, and San Francisco, the last of which is in the planning stage, Getty, Bilbao, and of course, the new Jewish museum of Berlin, to name but a few.

5. **Audiences.** The principal audience for Jewish museums in America, and even more so in Europe, is non-Jews. What an opportunity to achieve Goethe's dream for communication across borders and peoples. There are, however, a myriad of problems inherent in doing this, not the least of which is the difficulty in constructing exhibits and educational programs that contain many layers so that they can be effective for Jews who are Judaically well-educated, Jews who are not, and non-Jews, to delineate the audiences in but one of many possible ways.

6. **Market Frenzy.** President von Weizsäcker's son may have been ahead of his time in his love for comic books. Disneyland is now the paradigm for successful museums both in Europe and America. People now ask: Who is your architect? What kind of shop do you have? Does your café serve good and interesting food? And not, How effective are your exhibits and educational programs? It is difficult to focus attention on important and complicated topics when in cities like Chicago, the most-attended "museum" is the Nike store.

7. **The Collection.** We are running out of quality collections, and when art and artifacts are put on auction, the prices garnered for important objects are prohibitive for most museums. This condition has raised anew the question about whether a museum needs a collection, or are we better off with copies. As we deal with topics such as memory and memorialization there is a difference in touching an object that was manufactured the month before from touching objects that were used by our ancestors.

8. **Education.** The function of the Jewish museum is to engage in divine service. For Judaism, the highest divine service is study, learning, education. Therefore, our institutions are neither "Temples of Muses," nor "treasure-houses," nor warehouses, but schoolhouses. Not collecting, not exhibition, but education is our primary mission. Therefore, the appropriate criterion for evaluating the success or failure of our institutions is not how extensive our collections might be, nor how well we exhibit what we have, but how well we educate. We need to address ourselves to a large audience of voyeurs, but more importantly, we must find ways to engage learners. This is our criterion for success. This criterion is expanded if we include in our definition of "success" the ability to cross the borders among peoples and cultures.

In this world of disappearing borders, particularly because of advancements in communication technology, we have new opportunities for utilizing the museum for creative and exciting visual education. How we respond to this opportunity is a fundamental question at the center of internal and external museum meetings throughout the world.

NOTES

1. Byron L. Sherwin, "Faith as Memory," *Commitment and Commemoration* (Chicago: Exploration Press), 96.

2. Abraham Joshua Heschel, *Man Is Not Alone* (Philadelphia: Jewish Publication Society, 1951), 162–63.

3. Sherwin. For a more thorough discussion of this topic, see his paper: "Temple of Muses, Temple of Moses, or Galleries of Learning— Critical Problems of Jewish Museum Education," presented at CAJM meeting in Chicago, Spertus Institute, 1989.

CONCLUSION

Why Germany Remains Divided[1]

Andreas Glaeser

The mass media in Germany greeted the tenth anniversary of the fall of the Berlin Wall in the autumn of 1999 with a wave of reports about the state of the relationship between East and West Germans. Their relationship was at this time entering its tenth year under the common roof of a unified republic. The diagnosis advanced in these reports on East-West relations was—by and large—negative, attesting to an unabated, possibly even increased level of estrangement and incomprehension between the two main parts of the German citizenry. Thematically these reports were echoing, in an almost uncanny manner, a much earlier wave of media coverage that followed on the heels of political unification in October 1990. Then, the freshly unified polity was described for the first time as culturally divided, a division that was aptly captured in the image of the "walls in the minds of people" which had supposedly supplanted the Berlin Wall. If Germany today looks no more integrated than Germany nine years ago, if the division is felt as strongly as ever in spite of a set of federal policies which avow integration as their explicit goal, the question of why this division endures is of central importance. In the following pages, I will outline an answer to this question by showing how the organizational form of unification by accession, cultural differences which have emerged in forty years of life in radically different social systems, the ideological repertoire nourished in decades of Cold War confrontation, and the persisting uncertainties of Germans regarding their own Nazi past interact to produce continuing oppositional identifications between Easterners and Westerners. The linchpin of my argument is that in a situation of highly asymmetrical unification burdens, all of the factors just mentioned dovetail in such a way that the interaction between Easterners and Westerners typically proceeds in ways which lead to a misrecognition of Easterners' subjectivity. This misrecognition explains why Easterners continue to feel a lack of belonging in the unified German polity. The sure signs of this lack in belonging in spite of huge Western income transfers to the East are in turn the reason why Westerners feel that Easterners are ungrateful. I will unfold this argument in three steps: In the first two sections of this essay I will give an account of how the alienation between Easterners and Westerners has come about in the first place. The empirical basis for this part is ethnographic fieldwork I have undertaken in the state police departments of Brandenburg and Berlin between 1994 and 1996. Then, I will discuss why the alienation seems to persist, mostly by reference to the controversy over the future of the Palace of the Republic, East Berlin's former parliament cum sociocultural center. This part relies on ethnographic fieldwork I undertook in the summer of 1999 as well as on an extensive literature search. In conclusion, I will present a couple of suggestions for how the alienation between Easterners and Westerners could be eased.

From Political to Cultural Division[2]

The unification of Germany in 1990 proceeded on the assumption of an essential cultural unity of the German people in East and West. To be more precise: unification was acceptable to people in East and West Germany because the idea of the essential unity of the German people had sufficient resonance to legitimate the organizational form in which unification proceeded. These essentialist presuppositions are visible, for example, in the political rhetoric of the time, which was rife with

organicist metaphors of kinship and healing wounds. More importantly, however, they found their most vital expression in the relative
speed and form of unification, which proceeded in the historically
unique fashion of the voluntary, complete dissolution of one state (the
GDR) into the political, legal, and administrative framework of
another (the FRG).[3] Conditioned by the political fragmentation of
Germany in the nineteenth century, cultural essentialism as the consti-
tutive kernel of the German nation has a long tradition.[4] After the total
defeat of Nazi Germany in World War II, West Germany maintained
this tradition through a series of legal positions and foreign policy
measures that structured the relationship between the two German
states between their foundation in 1949 and their unification in 1990.
Among the most important ones are: the doctrine of sole representation and consequentially the refusal of the FRG to recognize the GDR
diplomatically; the demand for unification of the German people,
prominently placed at the beginning of the West German constitution,
which also self-confidently asserted that it had been promulgated for
the German nation as a whole; finally, the FRG's citizenship law, which
accepted only one all-German nationality and thus made it de facto
possible for East Germans visiting West Germany to obtain "their" West
German passport without any problems.

The essentialist stance of the Federal Republic with regard to
Germany as a whole softened during the era of *Ostpolitik*[5] and West
Germany's economic and cultural elites found it increasingly chic to
stress their elective affinities with like-minded friends in Paris and
Milan. Though they seemed to be basically losing interest in the GDR,
Ostpolitik actually supported sentiments of togetherness between many
people in both countries by facilitating millions of contacts between
relatives on both sides of the Iron Curtain. Thus, when the Wall fell,
Easterners and Westerners did in fact experience for a short moment
in time a feeling of real *communitas*. The immediate joy over the demise
of a dictatorship and an inhumane border regime seemed to corrobo-
rate the idea that the German nation was essentially one at heart and
unified in mind. Moreover, as Easterners left the GDR in droves to

settle in the FRG, and as election results showed a clear preference for unification by accession, old West German presumptions about being the one Germany seem to have been endorsed after all by the citizens of East Germany.

The demise of the old regime in the GDR and the currency union with West Germany began to create changes in the everyday lives of people in the GDR, which were wanted, even deeply desired. Above all, the availability of Western consumer goods as well as the freedom to travel were cherished additions to the GDR life, made possible by democratization and the availability of hard currency. The full impact and meaning of the unification by accession became palpable only, however, as Eastern lives were rendered increasingly more unpredictable in the aftermath of actual political unification when the political, economic, administrative, and juridical systems of the FRG became effective in the territory of the ex-GDR. Reasonable career expectations, based on established life trajectories, were suddenly invalidated, as many Easterners' professional qualifications became questionable, and labor markets began to work under conditions and according to rules different from anything East Germans had known. Employment itself, seen as a right as well as a duty in the GDR and never of any concern in what used to be a full-employment economy, was suddenly in danger of disappearing, as the East German economy was collapsing at a rapid pace.[6]

More importantly, the sweeping, wholesale adoption of Western institutions firmly established everything Western as a norm to which everything Eastern as deviant from this norm had to aspire. Any encounter with things Western identified Easterners as Easterners, and thus also as wanting and in need of adjustment. This is not only true for working life in now newly reorganized, that is, Westernized organizations but it permeated everyday life down to the consumption of ordinary goods:[7] the exercise of a myriad of everyday practices identified Easterners as deficient performers. Moreover, the increasing intensity of encounters between Easterners and Westerners, their efforts to work together on joint problems, made it patently clear that not only the way in which things are done were different in both countries, but also the ways in which people thought differed in significant ways. Thus, the essentialist presuppositions of the unification process were debunked as illusions in the daily encounters between Easterners and Westerners, which testified to profound differences in culture.

The Berlin Police, for Example[8]

The fate of East Berlin's former People's Police officers may exemplify what unification meant for many ordinary East Germans.[9] Their experiences can also illustrate why many Easterners still have very ambiguous feelings about their belonging in unified Germany, in spite of the fact that almost nobody would wish for a reinstitution of the GDR. It is one thing to reject the GDR but quite another to identify with the FRG. It is precisely Easterners' continuing reservation of positive feelings towards the FRG, that are at the core of the alienation between Easterners and Westerners. As I will show in this section, the Easterners' reservations have deep roots in the daily encounters with Westerners.

Although both police forces jointly staffed several working committees in summer 1990 to organize unification, at the end of the day, unification was, following the accession model for Germany as a whole, planned and executed unilaterally by the West Berlin Police. Beginning with unification day, all commanding positions in Eastern Berlin were staffed with Western officers, relegating Easterners basically to subaltern functions. In addition, all Easterners were individually reviewed for continued employment in the force. The standards for these reviews were set by Westerners, comparing Easterners to what would be expected of Westerners serving in the same position at the same rank. The Eastern police training was, curriculum hour for curriculum hour, compared to Western police training, and whatever didn't correspond was deemed irrelevant. Moreover, the careers of all officers were scrutinized individually for signs showing an especially strong commitment to the communist regime in East Germany to determine whether continued employment in a "democratic police" was acceptable. As a consequence of this review, all staff officers above the rank of major were dismissed, and all officers who were offered continuing employment were demoted by several ranks. Typically, Eastern officers thus found themselves after unification in the next lower career track (e.g., remaining staff officers became commissioned officers, commissioned officers became ordinary patrolmen). All officers had to undergo extensive retraining and they had to demonstrate their newly acquired knowledge in a reexamination showing that they would be able to interpret and enforce a new body of laws in accordance with the new liberal-democratic order of their new-old country. Finally, in keeping with the idea of producing incentives for Western companies to invest in Eastern Germany, wage rates in the five newly founded states on the territory of the former GDR were kept at 60 percent of Western levels with a gradual adjustment to Western standards. In the Berlin Police this led to the difficult situation that Eastern and Western police officers doing the same job were paid very different salaries.

The transition from the People's Police to the Berlin Police created a considerable amount of role insecurity among Eastern officers. Although Easterners at first expected police work in East and West to be roughly similar, everyday practices diverged significantly due to a very different division of labor in many parts of the police as well as due to a different understanding of the role of the law.[10] In addition to undergoing extensive retraining Easterners had to resolve themselves to accepting their Western colleagues as teachers even if they were much younger and much below the rank that Easterners had achieved in the People's police. Otherwise Easterners were sure to run afoul of their superiors who never failed to remind them in which way their actions were falling short of the Western norm. This of course does not at all mean that Westerners were unwilling to help; quite to the contrary, many Westerners made substantial efforts to help their Eastern colleagues. However, help was always provided according to the Western definition of the situation, that is Easterners were helped in their adjustment to meeting Western standards.

At the same time Westerners did not exactly receive Easterners with open arms.[11] Not only had Eastern and Western officers faced each other as enemies in decades of Cold War confrontation, but also Westerners typically suspected that their Eastern colleagues were deeply implicated in the old GDR regime. They believed that they were in all likelihood closely affiliated with the Stasi, the secret police of the former East Germany, which had become by that time the scapegoat for everything that was wrong with the GDR. Thus Easterners were looked upon by Westerners with strong moral reservations, which were frequently expressed in identifications between the GDR and Nazi Germany. The similarity between both regimes was for many Westerners evident in the outward similarity between Nazi and GDR institutions, ranging from a single party government and uniformed youth organizations to a goose-stepping military. In this vein, Western police officers also thought to discover reminiscences of Nazi Germany in the habitus of the People's Police, especially in its strict military order and demeanor. For Easterners with their antifascist self-understanding, the identifications between the GDR and Nazi Germany were of course a shocking provocation that they could not swallow easily, and to which they answered in turn by pointing to the continuities in personnel between Nazi Germany and the FRG. Thus, in effect, Eastern and Western officers exchanged once more the maligning rhetoric of the Cold War years, with the difference that the Westerners' position was bolstered now by ever-new revelations about suppressive actions in the former GDR.

Of course, the equation Westerners made between Nazi Germany and the GDR was only the tip of an iceberg of negative identifications of everything Eastern. There was barely any aspect of Eastern life that did escape Western satire and ultimately Western rejection, no matter whether talk turned to architecture, technology, social institutions, attitudes, styles, customs, or habits. For Easterners this was extremely hurtful because they were in part proud of what they considered major achievements of GDR society, especially the progress that had been made in reconstructing the country since the devastation of World War II. They had also lived in a land that had guaranteed work for everyone and had provided comprehensive state-run day care. In the face of this pride in their own achievements, which after all in many ways reflected the stories of their own lives, a particular style of Western denigration proved to be especially difficult to cope with for Easterners. Pointing to a crumbling facade in some Eastern street, Westerners would say, for example, "This looks like the West looked in the 1950s," or they would deride the latest People's Police technology as dernier cri of Western times long since past. The constant belittling of the East by Westerners often took the form of a temporal displacement in the sense that the Eastern present was identified with a Western past of several decades ago. What made this particular Western strategy so effective is that due to Easterners' own (socialist) ideology of progress, which placed a high value on economic and technological improvements, Easterners became unwitting coconspirators in the Westerners' denigration of the East. Easterners, at least at the beginning deeply impressed by Western wealth and Western technology, could not help but to assent to Westerners' judgements.

An especially important aspect of the Westerners' distemporalizing identifications is that they implicitly recommended a clear-cut blue-print of development for Easterners: a repetition, a reliving of Western history, ideally in fast-forward mode. This distemporalization strategy again resonates with an essentialist image produced in the West during the Cold War era that juxtaposed the vast majority of ordinary people in the GDR to the communist rulers and their apparatchiks. While the mass of ordinary people were thought of as being like Westerners, the apparatchiks were believed to keep the ordinary people from becom-ing "like every other German." Thus Westerners believed that ordinary Easterners had to constantly feign a socialist self behind which they maintained a true self that was much like the self of Westerners.

Although this presupposition of a shared cultural identity might have been true in the 1950s it certainly no longer held at the beginning of the 1990s. Forty years of life in different social, economic, and polit-ical systems, forty years of participation in a different set of discourses has indeed created distinctly different cultures in East and West Germany irrespective of the political allegiance of the people in ques-tion.[12] I can only hint at these differences here by sketching out two examples. Eastern and Western police officers mutually accused each other of not exhibiting the right attitude to work. As I started to analyze in which contexts and according to which criteria Easterners and Westerners identified each other as lacking a proper work ethic, I started to see that each side was operating with a different notion of time underpinning its evaluations. Westerners were using a notion of intensive time, which means that they praised those who performed work that was done well within as small a time span as possible. Easterners by contrast were using a notion of extensive time, which means that they praised those officers as good workers who demonstrated what was often referred to as "commitment." Commitment was shown in turn by accepting overtime work without complaint. It is particularly interesting that these uses of different criteria for assessing the morality of work performances resonate with fundamental organizational principles of capitalist and socialist economies.

Other cultural differences transpire from an analysis of the moral evaluations of the GDR, which were a constant sore point between Easterners and Westerners. Conversations about the wall and the Stasi have revealed interesting differences in the structure of moral reasoning between Easterners and Westerners. The core difference I observed between Easterners and Westerners was that Westerners made extensive use of a framework of individual rights, a strategy of assessment, which was almost completely absent from the deliberations of Easterners. Instead, Easterners used almost exclusively a sincerity framework for their moral evaluations of self, other, institutions, and the state. These differences in moral vocabulary had considerable consequences for the ability of Eastern and Western officers to morally judge the polity in which they had grown up. The rights framework, because it is organized in form of a catalogue, enabled Westerners to maintain a core identification with their state while critically evaluating parts of it. Easterners were, in the absence of a framework of individual rights, frequently thrown into the dilemma of either accepting the state or rejecting it.[13] Needless to say, such a dilemma is particularly hard to bear for a police officer. Cultural differences such as these fundamental disagreements about the proper ways to evaluate life do of course lead to many misunderstandings. They too greatly facilitate the erection of group boundaries between Easterners and Westerners, as everybody tries to find support among those who share a similar way of looking and judging.

A couple of numbers may also help to illustrate the situation of former People's Police officers. Of the 10,775 People's Police employees taken over by the (West) Berlin Police on October 3, 1990, a mere 5,115 were still employed by the department in summer 1995. In this time span about 900 of these officers left due to early retirement, and roughly 500 were dismissed for ties to the Stasi. It is hard to know what motivated the others, a staggering 40 percent of the initial group, to leave the police service. Some may have departed because they did not want to work for their former enemy; others might have been tired of police work; many might have dreaded the idea of having to go back to school; yet another group might have thought that they would not have much of a career prospect in the newly unified police anyway.

Although the experience of Berlin's former People's Police officers is in many ways unique, many features of their postunification life stories strike me as rather typical for the experience of the GDR population as a whole. There are the constant identifications of Easterners as Easterners, deeply inscribed in everyday life. There are the never-ending identifications of everything Eastern as either irrelevant, or negligible, backward, inferior, or morally dubious, identifications which are particularly hard to accept in their massive totalizing fashion if one has lived a significant portion of one's life in the GDR.

The Palace of the Republic

The everyday debates among Eastern and Western police officers not only reveal underlying thought patterns, they also simultaneously show how Easterners and Westerners understand and treat each other. Major public debates can serve a similar diagnostic function. Since unification by accession precluded a significant debate about the meaning of the unified German polity in the form of a public discourse about possible constitutional changes, the refashioning of one of its designated symbols, the capital city of Berlin, provides an ersatz forum in which important issues of political orientation can be raised. While the arguments over the Reichstag and the Holocaust Memorial principally raised issues of present-day Germany's relation to its own Nazi past, the debate about the future of the Palace of the Republic (henceforth "Palace") highlights the still problematic understanding between Easterners and Westerners. There are two parties to the dispute. One group advocates the preservation of the Palace in one form or another; the other group wants it torn down to make way for a reconstruction of the Hohenzollern Castle (henceforth "Castle"), which once stood where the Palace stands today. Although the fault lines in the debate about the future of the Palace are not entirely congruent with the East-West division, the support for the preservation of the Palace is predominantly based in the East, while the support for the reconstruction of the Castle is mostly a Western affair.[14]

The arguments of either side can be fully understood only by appreciating the history of the location for which a preserved Palace and a reconstructed Castle compete. The basic elements of the historical narrative are uncontroversial, which is the reason why it is possible to tell it first without direct reference to either party.[15] Located on an island created by the Spree river, sandwiched between the historical locations of the two founding communities of present-day Berlin, the medieval towns of Berlin and Cölln, the contested space can be considered the very center of historical Berlin. In the fourteenth century the Hohenzollerns made use of this strategic location from which they could easily control both towns by building their first Castle there. Changes in military technology and the relative success of the Hohenzollerns prompted a first complete remodeling of the Castle in the Renaissance. During Brandenburg-Prussia's rapid ascent to great power status in the eighteenth and early nineteenth centuries, the Hohenzollerns aimed to express their freshly gained position in the European order of states by launching a series of ambitious construction projects that eventually transformed the small, insignificant town of Berlin/Cölln into a respectable capital city. At the very beginning of this building boom, just in time to mark the newfound dignity of the Hohenzollerns as "kings in Prussia," there was another reconstruction and sizable expansion of their Castle. All the other buildings that today form the emblematic center of the city (the Brandenburg Gate, the museums, today's Humboldt University, etc.) were built after the Castle was reinvented in high Baroque style as a royal residence. Except for some minor additions and changes, including the erection of a dome above the main gate, the exterior of the Castle remained basically unaltered for the next 250 years. During the revolution of 1919, Karl Liebknecht, coleader of Germany's communist party, made an ill-fated attempt to proclaim a socialist German republic from one of the Castle's windows. During the Weimar Republic and the subsequent Nazi dictatorship the Castle was used as a public museum.

At the end of World War II, Berlin's city center, including the Castle and most of the other architectural showpieces in its vicinity, lay in ruins. Alas, unlike the other buildings representing Prussia's splendor, which were one by one carefully reconstructed by the GDR, the ruins of the Castle itself were blown up in 1950 in spite of a wave of protests from within and outside of East Germany. In addition to shying away from the enormous cost of the Castle's reconstruction, the GDR government apparently intended to leave a socialist imprint on Berlin's cityscape, and the Castle clearly stood in the way of these plans. For many years, the GDR did not have the economic wherewithal to do anything with the vast space emptied by the destruction of the Castle other than to use it for mass demonstrations. Later plans to build a central government building at this site failed to materialize both for lack of a convincing design that did not smack of Stalinist grandiosity as well as for want of funding.[16] When Erich Honecker succeeded Ulbricht in the early seventies, the need to find a new abode for East Germany's parliament was combined with the idea to build a sociocultural center (*Kulturhaus*) right in the middle of Berlin. Planning for this project to build a "Palace of the Republic" in the high modernist

184

style of the time began in 1973. In 1976 the Palace was opened, housing a multiplicity of performance spaces, including a technologically unique "Grand Hall," several restaurants, a youth club and bowling alleys under the same roof as the plenary hall of the parliament, which, since it was so rarely in session, was mostly used as a convention facility. Between its opening and its closure the Palace received 70,000 visits; it housed 20,000 different events ranging from Communist Party congresses to dance performances, symphony concerts, jazz sessions, cabaret evenings, and balls. In late summer 1990, the first freely elected parliament of the GDR decided to close the Palace due to asbestos poisoning. After having sold off all of the Palace's interior furnishings and putting a complete stop to all maintenance activities, the government decided to go ahead with radical asbestos removal, which will basically strip the interior of the Palace to its bare concrete and steel skeleton.

The core arguments advanced by the proponents of the reconstruction of the Castle are framed aesthetically and symbolically. Key to the argument of the Castle supporters is the fact that the emblematic center of Berlin was built after the Castle with a clear orientation toward the Castle. Thus, the Castle and its surrounding buildings form in their view an organic whole, a historical ensemble, which would remain essentially incomplete without rebuilding the Castle with at least its original facade and in its traditional proportions. Those who support the castle project often describe present-day vistas that include the Palace as disturbing the sense of balance and beauty that the original ensemble had achieved. Thus, it is argued for example that a walk from the Brandenburg Gate toward the Spree island ends today in the void of the square in front of the Palace; whole dimensions are perceived as too small and stylistically too much out of place to provide an aesthetically pleasing frame.

Interviews with proponents of the Castle's reconstruction show, however, that the aesthetic argument is intricately connected with other thoughts and feelings. There is most notably the craving for a center. On one level this is simply the longing for a beautiful inner city that will provide an orientation for Berlin's haphazard agglomeration of subcenters. This craving is particularly pronounced among West Berliners who were deprived of easy access to the center during the division of the city. Not surprisingly, then, Westerners' involvement in preservation and reconstruction projects in the district of Mitte (center) are in part also a way of repossessing the historical core of the city. The constant references to the city's center as "the living room of Berlin" *(die gute Stube Berlins)* make clear how these Westerners experience GDR buildings often as the illegitimate leftovers of an unwanted intruder.[17] Their scorn for GDR architecture is particularly pronounced with regard to the Palace, which is seen as the illegitimate consequence of the "cultural barbarism" of blowing up the Hohenzollern Castle.

On another level, however, the craving for a beautiful historical center is also the longing for an admirable tradition that can serve as an anchor for collective identities. Many proponents of a Castle reconstruction find such anchors embodied in the magnificent centers of other European capitals—most notably Paris, Rome, and London— and they wish very much that Berlin would be more like these cities in rendering the cultural achievements of their nation sensuously accessible in its marvelous architecture. Encapsulated in this craving for an admirable tradition is a rejection of the international style of architecture, which for many supporters of the Castle is the antithesis of an identity-generating form of spatial expression. To them, modern architecture is fungible and faceless, unable to grasp what is specific to Berlin, specific to Germany. This rejection of aesthetic modernism can, however, not be fully understood without seeing what aesthetic modernism meant in the lives of many Westerners. Amidst the debris of World War II, in face of the horrors of the Holocaust, aesthetic modernism seems to have had for many Castle advocates the lure of a clean, fresh beginning. Alas, the fiction of a clean slate came at least partially at the price of a wholesale rejection of tradition. While explaining how they have come to advocate for the Castle's reconstruction, they describe how the devastation of World War II and the guilt over Nazi atrocities had led them in the 1950s and 1960s to reject traditional forms in favor of modern ones. Modern architecture, Castle advocates argue today, has amplified the devastation that World War II wrought on Germany's cityscapes: the tales of the community, the continuity of its history are no longer visible to the flaneur. By reconstructing the Castle they hope to correct what appears to them now as the "sins of their youth," thus helping to bring Berlin and Germany back in touch with their own positive tradition, a tradition unscathed by World War II and the Holocaust.

The arguments of the Castle proponents are cast from a Western perspective, from Westerners' experiences of history, and with Western values in mind. The biographies of East Germans and the history of the GDR are a disturbing, annoying aside in the visions of Western Castle proponents for a renewed city center. Thus, Easterners' activities supporting preservation of the Palace of the Republic are quickly written off as GDR nostalgia, or worse, as the untenable ideological commitments of people incorrigibly devoted to a dictatorial regime.[18] Many East Berliners do indeed have tender feelings for the Palace, based in fond memories of the times they spent there attending performances, celebrating a "round" birthday with friends, or taking part in the many educational events sponsored by the Palace.[19] Thus, the Palace evokes many positive associations, rendering the building a physical anchor for the good memories of the GDR past.

The Palace with its many offerings, with its open hallways freely accessible to anybody anytime, was entirely unique in East Berlin, and it is probably fair to say that the Palace was East Berlin's social center, the closest thing East Germany ever had to an Italian piazza. This is not to deny, of course, that this space was closely controlled by the state, that everything that ever happened there was carefully censored; but it is probably also true that it is the space where the state was willing to cater most visibly to the tastes of its citizens. Thus, many older East Berliners feel that their life stories are closely connected with the Palace, and it is also by virtue of the Palace's function as anchor for positive memories that they would hate to see it destroyed. As this is not the rejection of the present in favor of an idealized past, it can hardly be called nostalgia. Rather it is the Easterners' desire to see their identities rooted in the spatial arrangements in which they live. As such it is the flip side of Westerners' desire to see themselves reflected in Eastern spaces by removing to the degree possible reminiscences of the GDR past.

Easterners' argument for the preservation of the Palace has a range of additional dimensions that warrant consideration. For many of them the Palace was one of the most important examples of public property, and they feel that the Palace was theirs, in part because of the sacrifices they made for its construction (for example, by accepting delays in the execution of public housing programs caused by the Palace). They also feel that the Palace, especially the multifunctionality of its Grand Hall—designed to adjust to various audience sizes, while minimizing the distance between viewer and stage—was a real technological accomplishment, one that still evokes a sense of pride in them. Unlike the Eastern police officers' comparison between People's Police and Berlin Police technology, Palace proponents' comparison between the Palace's Grand Hall and all other comparable halls in Berlin decisively comes down in favor of the Palace. Here they see proof yet again that Westerners are absolutely unable to look with an open mind toward Eastern accomplishments, exhibiting a readiness to destroy anything Eastern simply for the fact of its being Eastern. In this way, the debate about the future of the Palace has for many of them become a symbol of the way in which they see themselves treated within unified Germany.

In contrast to the aesthetically centered argument of the Castle proponents, Palace advocates are primarily concerned with the use of the location and the building. Above all, argue Palace proponents, Berlin's center must be kept open and accessible, it must remain a true public space, one that remains inviting to all—whatever their tastes or economic standing—a place where it is possible for anybody and everybody to meet. They think it would be a real setback if commercial or governmental interests reigned at a location that has provided them with such a sense of belonging. This is all the more important since many East Berliners feel already priced out of the center of the city. They acutely feel that the posh shops springing up along Friedrichstraße as well as the chic new restaurants and cafés are not for them, but rather for affluent Westerners; that the price levels they can no longer afford are intentionally employed to create social differentiation. Thus they are especially wary of the Castle proponents' general approach, which takes departure from the facade of the building while short shrifting questions of use and accessibility. Since the government has flatly refused to dedicate federal funds to a reconstruction of the Castle, private investors would have to be won over in order to launch the project. Private investors, however, reason the Palace supporters, would need a sizable return on their investment, which is only attainable by privatizing the use of the building to a considerable extent. Accordingly they tend to reject utilization proposals centering on conference facilities and a hotel.

Especially younger Palace advocates, who participate in the battle not for the building itself but mainly for the use of the space, are struck by the lack of ideas for a visionary use of Berlin's most hotly contested piece of land in the plans proposed by the Castle supporters. In clear distinction from these proposals, many of them see in the tradition of the *Kulturhaus*—a type of sociocultural center[20] with roots in Germany's labor movement—a platform that could be used to reinvent a reopened, possibly reconfigured Palace. This would be Berlin's version of the Centre Pompidou and could become a significant site for the exchange of ideas, a site worthy of occupying the center of the city.

In the controversy over the future of the Palace of the Republic, as in the daily interactions of Eastern and Western police, different ways of analyzing problems, different styles of thinking driven by different value hierarchies reveal cultural differences between East and West. One can see that a primary concern for the use of space contrasts with a preoccupation over its aesthetic appearance; a strong sense of public property compares with a search for private investment models. Where Palace and Castle proponents concur, however, is in their desire to belong in the center of Berlin. Alas, their different cultures and different histories create very different understandings of how this belonging should find physical representation.

For an understanding of the sources of alienation between Easterners and Westerners, the ways in which the contending parties take note of each other are particularly interesting. If both sides of the debate are asked to portray each other it quickly becomes clear that Palace supporters typically know much more about the arguments of Castle proponents than the other way around. There are probably two main causes for this asymmetry. Castle proponents, embedded in the political structures and journalistic networks of West Germany, have a much easier time ensuring that their message gets heard both by the people who matter in political decision making as well as by the mass of the population. Thus, the Castle proponents have succeeded in inserting their ideas about the future of the contested Spree island location into the official government-sponsored permanent exhibition on the future of Berlin. Their project is presented there right next to the approved models and plans for the reconstruction of government buildings, thus giving the Castle reconstruction the aura of an officially decided, already approved project. This asymmetry in the access to power also makes clear why the Palace proponents need to know more about the Castle proponents than the other way around: if they want to be effective, they have to maneuver in a world informed by the cultural presuppositions shared between Castle proponents and the powers that be. In other words, they have to play according to Western rules in a Western game, which is not traditionally theirs.[21]

Conclusions

The two case studies of East-West encounters analyzed in this paper, the unification and work-life of the Berlin Police, as well as the public debate about the future of the Palace of the Republic, provide a window into the causes of persisting oppositional identifications between Easterners and Westerners. The common thread that runs through both cases is this: Unification by accession has solidified and in part even sanctified Western Cold War understandings of the GDR and its inhabitants. Even more importantly, unification by accession has turned all East-West encounters into interactions that proceed according to Western rules and Western standards. Easterners are thus not only permanently identified as Easterners, but worse, they are in Westerners' eyes identified as deficient performers in need of adjustment. Through unification by accession Westerners have attained a structural and ideological position that exerts little pressure on them to think about Easterners as equal partners with a different history and with a different culture. While Easterners are forced by the same structural conditions to make a serious attempt to understand Western ways, Westerners' empathy for Easterners is hampered by the attribution of moral guilt to Easterners for their silent toleration if not active support for a dictatorship. This is read by Westerners into every Eastern defense or praise of the GDR. The emotional force of these moral attributions is only comprehensible in terms of Westerners' own insecurities about the degree to which they have come to terms with the specters of Germany's Nazi past. This dovetailing of traditions, ideologies, anxieties, and structural conditions has lead to a situation in which Westerners, including the political elites and the FRG state bureaucracy, constantly fail to recognize the full subjectivity of Easterners. In the language of the theory of dialogue[22] one would have to say that Westerners, and formerly Western and now all-German institutions, fail to treat Easterners as equal partners in dialogue in a situation that might be characterized as one of structural misrecognition.

This aggravation of the already enormous task of adjusting to a completely new world has hurled Easterners into painful status inconsistencies and uncertainties. Such persistent misrecognition makes it hard for Easterners to feel at home in the FRG even though most of them have attained a standard of living they could have only dreamt of in the GDR. Since this enormous surge in the standard of living in Eastern Germany is unthinkable without the large transfers from West to East, Westerners expect gratitude, which they want to see in

Easterners' expressions of happiness as citizens of the FRG. Alas, although unification was materially a success it has created many serious problems for Easterners. Thus, they wonder what precisely it is that they ought to be grateful for. Moreover, gratitude is hard to show in a situation of asymmetry of power and wealth and it is tantamount to self-depreciation in a situation of misrecognition.

Germany will remain divided as long as East Germans are not treated by West Germans as equal partners in dialogue. In other words Germany will remain divided as long as West Germans are unwilling to accept Easterners as equal partners on the basis of their full subjectivity rather than by virtue of their assimilation to Western standards. This must include a recognition by Westerners that Easterners are different, that forty years of life under very different circumstances have created appreciably different habits, different ways of approaching problems, other ways of thinking. This also includes a recognition that Easterners have their own history irrespective of how much this history is fraught with the active maintenance and passive toleration of a dictatorial regime. Thus, this history must not be looked at by Westerners as if it were best forgotten; rather, it needs to be incorporated into a public, plural vision of what it means to be a citizen of the Federal Republic of Germany.

The task of dialogue, the task of accepting the full subjectivity of the other, is closely tied to the ability to listen, and to be in the end ready to change in the encounter with the other. In addition, it is particularly this listening and the readiness to change through the touch of the other that has been continuously missing in East-West encounters. Unification by accession would not have had the divisive effect of normalizing everything Western while measuring everything Eastern as deviant from it if only Westerners had been graced with more substantial amounts of modesty, if they had been more prepared to recognize the shortcomings of their own system. Such modesty might have driven them to listen more closely to Easterners who, as keen observers of this new system, raise interesting, substantive questions about its nature, thus exposing some of the self-contentedness of the

Western society, economy, and polity. It is smug, for example, to brush aside Easterners' questions regarding the freedom of speech at the workplace; it is self-righteous to slight their bewilderment over Western pressures to find market-driven solutions for the center of Berlin. Easterners' puzzlement over many aspects of the Western system could be used as a starting point to think seriously about democratic reforms. This potential for reform in a dialogue between East and West, a dialogue that must encompass a serious reflection about Germany's two dictatorships while avoiding self-congratulatory attributions of guilt, could indeed provide valuable impulses for reinvigorating the democratic process in Germany.

NOTES

1. The research for the first two sections of this paper was made possible by a much-appreciated grant from the Program for the Study of Germany and Europe, Center for European Studies, Harvard University.

2. For a much fuller treatment of the argument presented in the following two sections please see Andreas Glaeser, *Divided in Unity: Identity, Germany, and the Berlin Police* (Chicago: University of Chicago Press, 2000). Based on extensive ethnographic fieldwork in the Berlin and Brandenburg police departments, this volume systematically explores the cultural differences between East and West Germans, while tracing East-West boundary building through policy decisions and everyday life with the help of a hermeneutic theory of identity construction.

3. The alternative path to unification, the election of a joint constitutional assembly, was soundly defeated in the first free East German elections of March 18, 1990, when conservative parties advocating unification by accession prevailed over the Social Democrats and the civil rights movement in the GDR who favored reconstitution.

4. See for example Rogers Brubaker, *Citizenship and Nationhood in France and Germany* (Cambridge, MA: Harvard University Press, 1992), and Liah Greenfeld, *Nationalism: Five Roads to Modernity* (Cambridge, MA: Harvard University Press, 1992).

5. See for example Timothy Garton Ash, *In Europe's Name: Germany and the Divided Continent* (New York: Vintage, 1993).

6. Even with the help of extensive government-subsidized employment programs, the unemployment rates in East Germany soared to well above 15 percent, reaching much higher rates in particularly hard-hit areas. For a recent assessment of the economic consequences of unification see Charles Maier, *Dissolution: The Crisis of Communism and the End of the GDR* (Princeton, NJ: Princeton University Press, 1997).

7. Compare especially Glaeser, *Divided in Unity,* on work, and Daphne Berdahl, *Where the World Ended: Re-Unification and Identity in the German Borderland* (Berkeley: University of California Press, 1999).

8. The Berlin Police was chosen as a fieldsite to study processes of identity construction between East and West Germans mainly because the Berlin Police is one of the few organizations in unified Germany where East and West Germans collaborate not only vertically but, due to the extensive mixing of officers, also horizontally within the same organizational hierarchy.

9. Although what follows pertains exclusively to the Berlin Police as far as the precise procedure is concerned, the magnitude of change, the upheaval in life experienced is not untypical for what happened to many East Germans. In many ways, the public sector employees were even privileged, because their risk at becoming unemployed was much lower than the risk faced by employees of what would become the private sector in East Germany.

10. With a few exceptions, Western policing affords the individual officer with much more independence. In addition, in spite of superficial similarities, socialist understandings of law are fundamentally different from liberal interpretations of law in that the former emphasizes substantive rationality while the latter stresses procedural (formal) rationality.

11. Of course, Easterners had reservations against Westerners as well. Alas, given the institutional structure of the situation their reservations were not backed by institutional power, rendering their reservations more into a "take it or leave it" choice.

12. Members of the GDR opposition were deeply formed by this culture too. Thus, sympathizers and opponents of the GDR regime frequently share their sense of frustration produced by encounters with Westerners.

13. The reliance on sincerity as key moral value has thrown People's Police officers into a serious double-bind situation, because their own personal desires (e.g., to meet Western relatives, or to watch Western television) clashed in significant ways with their commitment to their roles as police officers (who were as such forbidden to meet Western relatives and to watch Western television). For a detailed analysis of this problem see the chapters "Challenging Sincerity" and "Individual Rights and the Morality of States" in Glaeser, op. cit.

14. Some former members of the civil rights movement in the GDR have become advocates for a reconstruction of the Castle; some Western intellectuals and art historians arguing from the perspective of monument preservation abhor the idea of a reconstructed Castle, favoring instead a preservation of the Palace as an authentic monument.

15. My most important source for the history of the Hohenzollern Castle is Goerd Peschken and Hans-Werner Klünner, *Das Berliner Schloß* (Frankfurt am Main: Propyläen, 1982), as well as Renate Patras, *Das Berliner Schloß von 1918 bis 1950* (Berlin: Verlag für Bauwesen, 1992). The sources for the history and activities at the Palace of the Republic are Heinz Graffunder, *Der Palast der Republik* (Leipzig: Seemann, 1977); Bruno Flierl, "Das Kulturhaus in der DDR," in *Städtebau und Staatsbau im 20. Jahrhundert,* ed. Gabi Dolff-Bonekämper and Hiltrud Kier (München: Deutscher Kunstverlag, 1996); and Heinz Günter Behnert, *Palast, Palazzo: 1973 | 1997* (Berlin: edition bodoni, 1997).

16. See on this point also Bruno Flierl, "Der Staat in der Mitte Berlins," in Architektenkammer Berlin, *Architektur in Berlin: Jahrbuch 1993 / 1994* (Berlin: 1994).

17. Similar reactions are typical also for people born in some East German towns, who fled the GDR early on, and who now find any kind of changes in the cityscape effected during GDR times highly disturbing, as the unfamiliar construction undermines their feelings of belonging.

18. This reproach again resonates with that leveled against incorrigible Nazis in the debate about the proper consequences to be drawn from Germany's Nazi past.

19. See also Kirstin Heidler, ed., *Von Erich's Lampenladen zur Asbestruine: Alles über den Palast der Republik* (Berlin: Argon, 1998), and Behnert, *Palast, Palazzo.*

20. For a history of the *Kulturhaus* tradition in the GDR see Simone Hain, *Die Salons der Sozialisten: Kulturhäuser in der DDR* (Berlin: Ch. Links Verlag, 1996), and Bruno Flierl, "Das Kulturhaus in der DDR," in

Städtebau und Staatsbau im 20. Jahrhundert, ed. Dolff-Bonekämper and Kier.

21. The organizational form of both groups is telling in this regard. While Castle proponents are organized in one registered association with tax deduction privileges, the support for the Palace is fragmented into at least four different groups, none of which are legally registered, and thus none of which are eligible for tax deduction privileges.

22. Understood here in the tradition of Martin Buber, *Ich und Du* (Stuttgart: Philip Reclam jun., 1995); Mikhail Bakhtin, *Problems of Dostoevsky's Poetics*, ed. and trans. Caryl Emerson (Minneapolis: University of Minnesota Press, 1984); and Hans-Georg Gadamer, *Wahrheit und Methode: Grundzüge einer philosophischen Hermeneutik*, Ergänzungsband (Tübingen: J.C.B. Mohr [Paul Siebeck], 1990).

CONTRIBUTORS

Henryk Broder is a columnist and correspondent for *Der Spiegel*. He is one of the most important essayists in Germany, standing in a long tradition of Jewish commentators on the German scene from Ludwig Börne via Karl Kraus to Kurt Tucholsky.

Tom L. Freudenheim is former deputy director of the Jewish Museum in Berlin. A long-time figure on the cultural landscape in Washington and New York, he is one of the old-new Americans in the new Berlin.

Sander L. Gilman is Henry R. Luce Distinguished Service Professor of the Liberal Arts in Human Biology at the University of Chicago and author of *Jews in Today's German Culture*.

Andreas Glaeser is an assistant professor of sociology at the University of Chicago and the author of *Divided in Unity: Identity, Germany, and the Berlin Police*.

Todd Herzog is an assistant professor of German at the University of Cincinnati. He recently completed his Ph.D. at the University of Chicago with a dissertation on criminality in Weimar culture.

CONTRIBUTORS

Barbara John is secretary for foreigners of the senate of Berlin. Her position in the city government was created when Richard von Weizsäcker was the mayor of West Berlin.

David Levin is an associate professor in the Department of Germanic Studies at the University of Chicago and author of *Richard Wagner, Fritz Lang and the Nibelungen: The Dramaturgy of Disavowal.*

Dagmar C. G. Lorenz is professor of German at the University of Illinois at Chicago and the author of *Keepers of the Motherland: German Texts by Jewish Women Writers.*

Helmut Müller-Sievers is an associate professor in the Department of German and Director of the Alice B. Kaplan Center for the Humanities at Northwestern University.

Saskia Sassen is a professor in the Department of Sociology at the University of Chicago and the author of *Guests and Aliens.*

Peter Schneider is one of Germany's preeminent contemporary novelists. His novels about the new and the old Germany include *The Wall-Jumper: A Berlin Story.*

Howard A. Sulkin is president of Spertus Institute of Jewish Studies and chairman of the board of the Council of the Parliament of the World's Religions.

Monika Treut is an independent filmmaker. Her films include *Seduction: The Cruel Woman, Didn't Do It for Love,* and, most recently, *Gendernauts.*

Richard von Weizsäcker is the former mayor of West Berlin and president of the Federal Republic of Germany.

INDEX

Aguirre, the Wrath of God 120
Aimee und Jaguar 125
American Reform Judaism 3
Anderson, Sascha 11
Architecture
    and nature 38
    humane concept of 31
    in Chicago 37–38
Aspen 5, 17
The Aspen Idea 20
Aspen Institute 5, 27, 39
Ataman, Kutlug 128–129
Auschwitz 86

Beethoven, Ludwig van 82
Begnini, Roberto 161
Benjamin, Walter 105, 145
Berlin 7–9, 14, 145, 157, 158, 183
Berlin Alexanderplatz 121
Biermann, Wolf 11
The Black Atlantic 15, 20
Black Dogs 157, 164
The Blair Witch Project 127
The Blue Angel 119
Borders 12–14
Borgese, Giuseppe Antonio 4, 27

Börne, Ludwig 109
Bosnia 85–86
Brandenburg 11
Brandt, Willy 11
Broder, Henryk 12, 18, 106
Bruchstücke. Eine Kindheit 1939–1948
    107
Bubis-Walser debates 160–161, 163
Buchenwald 10, 110

The Cabinet of Dr. Caligari 119
Canetti, Elias 157
Cannes 124
Carriere, Jean-Claude 126–127
Celan, Paul 157
Chesterton, G.K., 10
Chicago
    architecture 37–38
    German identity in 1–4
Citizenship laws 47, 101, 175
Cohen, Roger 20
Comedian Harmonists 125
Commissioner of Foreigners' Affairs,
    Office of 43
Congress of Vienna 32
Container Corporation of America 5, 27

INDEX

Conversations of Goethe 20

Daimler-Chrysler 84
Dana International 103
A Dangerous Friend 163
Derrida, Jacques 10, 20
Deutsches Historisches Museum 153,
    164
    "Einigkeit und Recht und Freiheit,
    Wege der Deutschen, 1949–1999"
    exhibition 153–154
Didn't Do It for Love 131
Dische, Irene 13–14
Displaced persons 151
*Displacement, Diaspora, and Geographies of
    Identity* 21
Döblin, Alfred 145
Doering, Zahava 159
Dogma 95 128

Eckardt, Ulrich 7
Education (in Germany) 91, 110
Eisenman, Peter 10, 100
Emerson, Ralph Waldo 31
The End of History and the Last Man 20
Engels, Friedrich 26
Euro 14–15, 32, 81, 82
Euro-citizen 81–83
European Union 16, 33–34, 51, 59–60,
    62, 63, 67, 72, 80–84, 110–111
    audiovisual policy of 126
    linguistic diversity in 83–84

Fassbinder, Rainer Werner 120–121,
    135
Female Misbehavior 132
Film industry
    and the Internet 127–128
    dominance of Hollywood in 118
    effect of digital technology on
    127–128
    funding of 118, 121–123
Filmkritik 123

Fischer, Fritz 9, 20
Flensburg 14
Fom winde ferfeelt 21
Francis Fukuyama and the End of History
    20
Frankfurt am Main 12
Frankfurt/Oder 35
Franklin, Benjamin 31
Freedom
    and democracy 36, 37
    of speech 36–37
Fried, Erich 11
Fukuyama, Francis 12, 20
Fuller, Margret

German-American Relations 1–4,
    30–31, 100, 148
German cinema
    and national historiography 132
    and other art forms 125–126
    compared with other European
    national cinemas 127
    documentary film 128
    effect of multiplexes on 122–123
    in the Weimar Republic 118–119
    in postwar Germany 119
    involvement of television in 122
    New German Cinema 119–121,
    124, 132
    New National German Cinema
    123–126
    success at the box office in 1990s
    124
    under National Socialism 119
German-Jewish relations 99–100, 107,
    147–152
German language 84, 90
German-Polish relations 34–35
Gide, André 28
The Gift of Death 10, 20
Gilroy, Paul 7, 15, 20
Global cities 53, 69, 70
Globalization 49–68, 111, 146

and perceptions of American cultural dominance 30
Goethe, Johann Wolfgang von 4–7, 10, 20, 25, 27–28, 38, 39, 47, 87, 90–94, 105, 107–110, 126, 143, 144, 148, 162, 168, 170
  and National Socialism 110
  as symbol of Germany 108
  autobiographic writings 90
  French opinions of 28, 30
  in academic criticism 91
  inability to write tragedy 93
  notion of *Weltliteratur* 29
  on German nationalism 27–28, 29, 109
  on the United States 28–29, 143–144
  support for emerging cultures 28
  theory of organisms 90
Goethe bicentennial celebration 4–5, 17, 25, 27, 39
Goethe Bytes 108
Goethe—le Grand Européen 28
Goethe Street (Chicago) 167
Gölz, Sabine 2, 20
Grand Prix d'Eurovision 103
Grass, Günther 2, 102
Grillparzer, Franz 107
Guillaume, Günther 11
Gulf War 102–103
Guthke, Karl 5, 20

Hamburg Institute for Social Research 9
Handke, Peter 103
Havemann, Robert 11
Heer, Hannes 9
Hegi, Ursula 2–3, 4, 16, 20
Hein, Christoph 103
Heine, Heinrich 107, 144, 155–156, 161
Herzog, Werner 120, 135
Heschel, Abraham Joshua 167–168
Hesse 11

Hilsenrath, Edgar 111
Hirsch, Emil 3
Hitler, Adolf 7, 10
Hölderlin, Friedrich 94
Holocaust 3, 10, 11, 12, 106, 144, 158
  debate over uniqueness of 150
  effect of on post–World War II architecture 187
  relationship of contemporary Germany to 9–10, 132, 146–147, 150, 151, 161
  relationship of post-1945 German Jews to 151
  representations of 161
Holocaust Memorial (Berlin) 10, 100, 106, 107, 161, 183
Honecker, Erich 185
Honigmann, Barbara 13
Horn, Guildo 103
Humboldt, Alexander von 86
Humboldt, Wilhelm von 89, 91
  philosophy of language 89–90
Hutchins, Robert M. 5, 25, 27
Hygiene Museum (Dresden) 155
  "Der Neue Mensch" exhibition 155
Hyman, Sidney 20

Immigration and ethnic diversity in Germany 12–14, 36, 43–48, 57, 71, 101, 106
Israel 147–148, 152

Jakob Littners Aufzeichnungen aus einem Erdloch 12, 20
Janka, Walter 11
Jarausch, Konrad H. 21
Jefferson, Thomas 31
Jelinek, Elfriede 111
Jens, Walter 102
Jewish studies
  comparison of programs in Germany and United States 148–149

INDEX

Just, Ward 1, 144, 163

Kant, Hermann 11
Kaspar Hauser
Kleist, Heinrich von 35, 94
Kluge, Alexander 120
Knight, Julia 134, 137
Koeppen, Wolfgang 12
Kohl, Helmut 9, 11
Kosovo 85–86, 105, 106
Kramer, Jane 150
Krieg der Illusionen 20
Krondorfer, Björn 3, 20

Lander, Jeanette 13–14, 111
Langlois, Henri 123
Last Words 20
Lavie, Smadar 15, 21
Das Leben ist eine Karawanserei 13, 21
Leitkultur 45
Leopardi, Giaccomo 38
A Letter without Words 158
Lewald, Fanny 109, 112
Lewenz, Lisa 158
Libeskind, Daniel 100
Lichtenberger, Henri 28
Liebknecht, Karl 184
Life Is Beautiful 161
Loehst, Erich 11
Lola and Bilidikid 128–129
Longfellow, Henry Wadsworth 31

The Man Who Was Thursday 10
Mann, Thomas 4
Männerpension 124
The Marriage of Maria Braun 120
Martenstein, Harald 12, 20
Marx, Karl 26
Maxims and Reflections 47
McEwan, Ian 157, 164
Memory 157–158
 and experience 158
Metropolis 119

Mickey Mouse 30
Milosevic, Slobidan 103, 104
Monnet, Jean 33
Müller, Hertha 13, 21
Museums
 and Jewish tradition 169, 171
 and memory 156, 159
 art and history museums compared
 159–160
 Jewish museums in Germany 153,
 156–157, 158–159, 160, 168
 Jewish museums in the United
 States 168–171
 relationship to museum visitors
 159
 role of 153, 169
My Father Is Coming 132

NAFTA 51, 55, 62, 63, 64–65, 67, 73
Naming laws 47
Napoleon 32
NATO 16, 26, 27, 85, 104, 150
Neo-Nazis 7, 101
Nosferatu 119

Oberhausen Manifesto 121
Ortega y Gasset, José 32
Ostalgia 15
Ostpolitik 175
Özdamar, Emine Sevgi 12, 13, 21

Paepcke, Walter Paul 5, 27
Palace of the Republic 7, 183–190
 debate over preservation of 183,
 185–190, 196
 site of 183–185
Plötzlich ist alles ganz anders 21
Police force 177–182
 attitude of officers toward work
 181
 differences between Eastern and
 Western technology 180
 retraining of Easterners in after

unification 177–178
suspicion by Westerners of officers of the former GDR 179

Qaiyum, Abdul 2
Querrelle 135

Rabinovici, Doron 111
Rathenau, Walther 8
Raulff, Ulrich 146
The Reader 161
Reisende auf einem Bein 21
Remembrance and Reconciliation 20
Renan, Erest 32
Retour a Berlin 30
Revolver 123
Reunification 11, 14–15, 16, 33, 35–36, 79–80, 92, 101–102, 105–106, 173, 174–177, 194
and the Berlin police force 177–182
and the Palace of the Republic 183–190
structural misrecognition and 191–193
Rock, Zé do 13, 21
Rohe, Mies van der 37
Rolland, Romaine 28
Rossini 124
Rostock 14
Rusch, Regina 21

Saarbrücken 14
Sadomasochism 117, 133–136
Sander, Helke 135
Santner, Eric 132, 137
Saures, André 28
Sayn-Wittnstein, Casmir Prinz zu 11
Schäubele, Wolfgang 9
Schiller, Friedrich 81, 93, 144
Schlink, Bernard 161
Schlörndorff, Volker 120
Schneider, Peter 18
Schtonk 125

Schulze, Ingo 14
Schweitzer, Albert 5, 39
Schwerin 14
Science and democracy 37–39
Seduction: The Cruel Woman 135
Sight and Sound
Simple Stories 14
Singer, Isaac Bashevis 157
Sloterdijk, Peter, 132–133
Slubice 35
Smithsonian Institution 154
Enola Gay exhibition 154–155, 160
Sohara's Trip 13
Sollors, Werner 16
Der Spiegel 105
Stalingrad 125
Stasi 106
Stein-Pyritz, Isabell 46
Stolpe, Manfred 11
Stones from the River 2
Stranded Objects 132, 137
Strasbourg 13
Strauss, Botho 94, 132
Swedenburg, Ted 15, 21
Syberberg, Hans-Jürgen 94, 133

Tabori, George 107, 111
Tearing the Silence 2–3, 20
Thierse, Wolfgang 8
Thirty Years' War 32
Thompson, Dennis F. 20
Thorough, Henry David 31
Thuringia 10, 15
Torkan 111
Treut, Monika 131–136
Trilling, Lionel 95
Trommler, Frank 16
Trotta, Margarete von 120
Tucholsky, Kurt 102

University of Chicago 4–5, 17, 25, 27
University of Virginia 31
Die unverhoffte Einheit 1989–1990 21

INDEX

Valéry, Paul 28
Viadrina 35
Virgin Machine 131

"The Wall in the Head" 14, 173
Walser, Martin 103, 132
Warsaw Pact 16
Weimar 6, 10, 92
Weimar Republic 7
Weizsäcker, Richard von 17, 43, 170
Wenders, Wim 120, 133
Wernder, das muß kesseln 124
Wilde, Oscar 11

Wilhelm II 7
Wilkomirski, Binjamin 107
Williams, Howard 20
Wilson, W. Daniel 108, 112
Winfrey, Oprah 2
Wolf, Arnold 3
Wolf, Christa 10–11, 102
Women and the New German Cinema 134, 137
World Trade Organization 49, 51

Yesterday Girl 120
Yiddish 157